ICE FISHING

ICE FISHING

Methods & Magic

Steven A. Griffin

STACKPOLE BOOKS

Published by
STACKPOLE BOOKS
Cameron and Kelker Streets
P.O. Box 1831
Harrisburg, PA 17105

Printed in the United States of America

10 9 8 7 6 5

Cover photograph by Dale C. Smith
Cover design by Tom Todd and Jan Scott

Library of Congress Cataloging-in-Publication Data

Griffin, Steven A.
  Ice fishing.

  Includes index.
  1. Ice fishing.   I. Title
  SH455.45.G75   1985   799.1′2   85-21959
  ISBN 0-8117-2407-7

Dedication

To the people in my life — Tom, Dale, Howard and Margaret, May, Myrtle, and Art — who've believed in the magic of ice. And to wife Mary Jo, who's shared and provided the magic of life; may our child tramp snowy footprints onto hundreds of lakes.

Contents

Introduction

It's mid-July and I'm fumbling with a tip-up. Sweat breaks on my brow and still I'm dreaming of wind-swept snow and numbed fingers. Bass fishermen are pulling 'hawgs' out of lush lake vegetation and I'm mentally sliding a bluegill across four-inch thick ice into which I've drilled a hole.

I'm not completely crazy, and I'm surely not alone.

Countless anglers pursue at least part of their fishing sport in winter. For some of them ice fishing is what they do to cope with ice formation over their favorite warmweather fishing spots. But for others, it's mysteriously different. Summer fishing is what I do in the "off" season, during those dreadfully long months between ice-out and freeze-up of my favorite lakes.

Seldom can you find faster fishing action than on a lake when it first freezes over. Never can you fry up a mess of panfish that tastes as good as that first ice-caught meal of early winter. And never — never — can you match the beauty and serenity of an ice-bound lake.

Maybe you already know all this. Perhaps we've compared notes on a frozen lake somewhere. If so, thanks for the tips you passed my way. Here are some tricks you might want to try.

Maybe, though, your ice fishing time has been limited by a lack of information. Or a fear that you'll break through the ice, or freeze solid. Or maybe just because you've never quite taken the time to try this sport.

Regardless, come along. New fisherman or veteran, in January or mid-summer. Turn a few pages. We're going ice fishing!

Fishing and, to an even greater extent, fishing regulations differ as one travels across ice country. Not only do rules change from state to province to state, they even change from lake to lake and season to season on the same lake! That makes it impossible for a book to provide you with all the information you need to stay on the good side of fishing law. And rather than do the disservice of leading you to believe otherwise, we've left the legal research to you.

Obtain a copy of the fishing regulations for the state or province in which you'll be doing your ice fishing, and read it closely. Watch for such restrictions as closed seasons, bans on live bait (especially minnows) and limits on the types of gear you can use. Ice shanties and snowmobiles are two other subjects regulated in varying degrees in each area.

Nor do we pretend to cover all the various ice-fishing strategies one can employ to take winter fish. That would require a series, not just one book.

This book divides ice fishing into general categories, and for each we discuss basic fishing methods that will take fish. You take it from there — adapting the methods, if necessary, to fit the fish and conditions you face. That's part of the fun of ice fishing, anyway — matching wits with your quarry.

And while there are subtle differences in fishing approaches across ice country, the magic of the sport is a common one. This book's main goal is to get you on the ice with the basic know-how required to taste success. There the magic will capture you.

Figure 1 — Sunrise finds an ice fisherman far offshore, his power auger throwing shards of ice into the early sunlight.

Chapter 1

Ice Fisherman's Sunrise

Sunrise is a good half-hour off, judging by the red, yellow and purple clouds huddled against the eastern horizon. An hour has passed since we left the car, shouldered loads of clothes and tackle, and trudged onto this big, frozen lake.

We checked the ice and know it's safe. So we made good time walking out, step after slippery step. More than one clumsy dance-step motion was made as horizontal ice juggled vertical anglers. Now we're about a mile offshore.

We're ready for some ice fishing, eager to take part in a sport that's the butt of altogether too many jokes and cartoons. Some non-fishermen and non-ice-fishermen think we're crazy, but that's okay. We really don't mind. We were here yesterday, too, and many of the jokesters would have envied the fat lake trout we carried off, two apiece.

Let's try for a replay. We'll use the same tip-ups, bait up with live smelt of about the same size. Over here's the hole through which the day's lunker, a lake trout of about 10 pounds, was extracted.

The trout shed a few drops of blood on the ice after its

1

ascent from 100 feet down, and those stains are still visible in the snow. I'm going to set one of my tip-ups in that lucky hole.

Our other partner is already hard at work with the power auger, glad now that he lugged it the long way out. In 15 minutes he'll have drilled enough holes for a day's wandering ice fishing.

You've come along to see just what this ice fishing stuff is all about, and it's up to me and my buddy to show you why we've made all this effort.

Part of the answer is that vivid sunrise and the solitude in which we're enjoying it. We're a good half-mile away from our nearest angling neighbors, and they're barely visible in the thin morning light. Spectral sunrise colors, glowing through ice shards spinning off the power auger present a pleasant blend of things human, natural and mechanical. I like, too, the crisp air that's filled our lungs and slightly numbed our hands. We'll get used to the cold, I promise, and your fingers will be capable of fighting and icing a lake trout when the time comes.

Three of us have set six tip-ups, the maximum allowed in Michigan. Some states allow their anglers fewer fishing lines, some more, but our two apiece will keep us busy enough.

Tip-ups, simply, are crossed sticks that support a reel underwater and a flag above the ice. They're connected by a mechanism that holds the springy flagstaff under tension. When a fish takes the bait and pulls line, the reel turns. That releases the flag which, now flying erect, signals the angler to action.

All six flags are now set, and the waiting has begun. We're hoping, of course, that the lake trout will cooperate as they have on so many memorable fishing days in the past. By the time this fishing session is over, you'll have heard about some of those days. We'll try not to exaggerate too much.

This post-dawn period is the coldest time of the day, as far as I am concerned. Each of us pulls one more time on the coat zippers and burrows our hands a little deeper into the mitts, trying to keep exposed flesh to a minimum. Cold as it is, though, I've a good hunch this is going to be a pleasant fishing day.

Work is far away, and we've only borrowed such trappings of civilization as needed for this sport: the car that brought us here, the clothes that hold in most of our warmth, the auger that drilled the holes, and the nylon fishing lines — one of which is now spinning off an underwater reel toward a retreating lake trout!

That's your tip-up! The flag is waving in the early-morning breeze, and I swear I can see the tip-up actually wobbling back and forth in the hole as the fish spins off line. The water beneath is 100 feet deep or more, and God only knows how long that flag has been flying. There's 150 yards of line on that tip-up, but I've seen lakers run that far and more; Let's get on over!

The fish is still running as the three of us huddle over the hole in the ice, trying to decipher from the spinning reel the actions and even the mood of the fish.

Here, take the line while it's slack and wait for the fish to snug it up. Toss those mittens aside, for this battle's to be fought bare-handed. When you can feel the fish, give the line one good tug to set the hook, then start bringing in line hand-over-hand, as the fish allows you to.

This is a classic lake trout fight. For a while he comes toward the hole fairly easily, then he's off on a stubborn run. You've always got to be ready to allow him to take line. Toward the end of the fight the fish may seem to be beaten, but be on guard as he approaches the hole. There's almost always one more burst of angry energy in store before the fish comes atop the ice.

Dale is backing up behind you, gradually winding back onto the tip-up reel the line you've won from the fish. We've found that helps us in several ways. For one thing the line doesn't lay tangled and snarled on the ice in the event a hard-running fish demands it back. If the fish runs, give Dale a yell; he'll make sure line pays freely from the tip-up. And when the battle's over, the tip-up will be ready for quick re-lowering for another try at a trout.

Fighting a fish this way, a handful of line at a time, gives you an appreciation for a yard of monofilament that you can never gain fighting a laker with a rod and reel.

Behind our backs the sun is rising a little higher and, now that your battle with the laker is nearly over, the yellow-gold rays of the sun shine on the fish's sides as it comes nearer the hole.

Until now we could tell only by the action that there was a fish on the other end of the line; this is our first sight of it. The mottled-gray appearance almost takes the breath away, so magically it appears. It seems to fade into view. And believe me, you'll never get over that magic, no matter how many lakers you ice.

When the fish nears the hole the angler's nerves often fray. Carefully bring the fish to the edge of the hole, then gently start its nose upward. I'll grab the trout by the gills or body, wherever I can find a handle. I wouldn't really mind if you were trying to grab a fish of mine, missed and knocked the fish off. But I'd sure hate to lose your first laker for you. There — I got'm! I've grabbed his gill plate and given him a toss and there he is, flopping a few last times in the snow a few feet away.

Go ahead, spend a few minutes admiring the eight-pound trophy you've taken. If we judged you right, you'll feel a twinge of regret as the laker's blood stains the snow. Take your time; we'll start setting back up.

It may well be an hour or more before there's more action, and I sure hope you don't mind. Like most anglers, we prize the sport more than the catch. We'll try every trick we know to boost and catch, and sit back and laugh if all those tricks fail. Most times, they don't.

Your hands look like they've finally warmed after the 10-minute, bare-handed, wet-line fight with the lake trout. You've even remembered to retrieve the mitts you tossed aside when the battle began. And your victorious grin has mellowed into an all-day smile.

Ice fishing is funny. The sport seems so strange to those

who have never tried it, so natural to those of us who love it. And believe me, it's possible to learn quickly to love it.

Dale Smith, now a long-time fishing partner, first bid me shake hands with 'serious' ice fishing. Dale and I had spent some mid-November deer hunting time together, and one day we went scouting for new hunting grounds, pulling into a state forest campground adjacent to a large piece of state-owned land. Through the camp flowed Black Creek, backed up by a dam on a large river several miles downstream. As a result of the dam, current in this creek is virtually nonexistent, and thus it freezes early. On this late-fall day the creek had frozen, and that short-circuited all our deer hunting plans.

At the sight of the frozen waterway Dale put all his other plans on the back burner. He rarely travels without a spud in the trunk of his car, at least from fall through spring. In an instant he had thrown a large rock onto the ice and, when it didn't even produce a crunch, he grabbed the spud. Tapping carefully he roamed out from shore, finally cutting a hole in the ice a few feet out. The ice was safe — better than three inches thick.

We immediately drove back to town and Dale collected a couple of light jigging sticks and a handful of jigging lures. At a nearby sporting goods store we bought a couple of dozen wax worms for bait. Summer-fishing fans too, we already had our fishing licenses. So in less than an hour we were back on the creek.

I watched the action from shore at first. Dale snuck out, cut a hole in the ice and, minutes later — while high-power deer rifles boomed in the distance and shoppers elsewhere examined Thanksgiving turkeys — he pulled a chunky bluegill onto the ice. Then another. When four or five nice 'gills flopped on the ice Dale urged me again to join him.

I grabbed a jigging rod and all the courage I could muster and stepped out from shore, walking carefully along the path Dale had taken. He quickly showed me how to set the tiny bobber at the proper depth, how to jiggle the rod lightly and detect a strike and, finally, how to ice a bluegill once it struck. More even than the bluegill, I was hooked!

All the way home that day, and for many weeks afterward, I bombarded Dale with questions. I wanted to learn all I could about ice fishing, and the sooner the better.

Patiently Dale fielded my many questions. Usually his answers were simpler than the inquiries. And maybe that's what I like best about ice fishing. It's a straight-forward sport. You can get just as fancy with your fishing gear as you like, but ice fishing remains a relatively simple game.

You can count on motorized vehicles to take you to your fishing spot, but walking's an infinitely better and safer idea. You can yank on a power auger and guide it quickly through a foot of ice or more, but a $15 spud will do the same job, even if it takes a little more work and time. You can assemble a fancy collection of tackle, but everything you really need will fit in a cast-off five-gallon plastic bucket, and you probably won't have $25 invested.

You do, however, need the desire to head onto the ice in the first place.

My very first ice fishing was inspired as much by hunger for food as by thirst for sport. Mary Jo (then my girlfriend and now, happily for me, my wife) and I were in college. Tuition, books and somewhat less-academic expenditures had deflated our budgets, and we'd grown so very tired of macaroni and cheese and spaghetti. When we heard that large perch were biting well through the ice of a small lake nearby, our imaginations cooked up a mess of perch fillets, bubbling in hot grease.

It turned out that the report was actually reversed. They were actually small perch in a large lake. We didn't mind, though. We threaded newly-purchased lines and lures down holes leftover by previous anglers, easing the hooks down into about 20 feet of water. The perch, mostly six-inchers and even smaller, inhaled the lures as soon as they fell. After two hours, a dozen line-tangles and even an early-spring rain, we'd filled a bucket with perch.

Cleaning the catch was the next chore, and I have to say

there were few among my fellow dormitory residents who approved of fish-filleting in the shared kitchen. They had thought us a little 'tetched' before, just for going ice fishing. They now viewed our sopping-wet, fish-cleaning reappearance as proof we were daft indeed.

But those tiny fillets, rolled in pancake flour and fried in hot oil, produced the single finest meal I've enjoyed in my life.

It still makes me hungry just to tell that story.

My wife and I were married for three full years before she ever saw Higgins Lake in an unfrozen state. It's rated one of my native Michigan's most beautiful lakes, and she thought it had probably earned that reputation in summer. I told her it was prettiest in winter, and I still don't know if she believed me.

Higgins is a big lake, plenty deep once you've ranged far enough offshore to where a drop-off falls about forty feet down in forty feet of walking. A similar drop further out breaks into more than 100 feet of water. Along those ledges roam the lake trout and splake (an interesting hybrid cross of lake and brook trout) that I love best.

We'd coaxed Mary Jo into joining us on Higgins Lake one winter day. We'd been taking trout with some regularity but never in what you'd call red-hot action. Three friends joined us as we walked out to the drop-off into 110 feet of water. We'd built snow castles the previous day to mark the best holes and kill some of the hours in which even the good holes didn't pay off.

We scattered to those holes and started setting tip-ups. "How deep is it here?" asked a friend who'd not fished this lake before. I told him a little more 100 feet. "But I have 150 feet of line out," he protested, "and still haven't hit bottom." A light went on in his head and his face broke into a rather foolish smile as he set the hook and fought a hungry trout to the surface.

The splake, eager for a meal, hadn't even waited for the minnow to reach bottom before engulfing it. Fred fought his fish while the rest of us laughed at the fast action. And before his fish came through the hole another flag was flying. Then another. For two hours the fish kept us busy chasing flags, fighting fish and re-baiting. We called it a day one short of the limit for all five anglers.

Not many ice fishing outings produce that kind of action. But similar experiences are relived on a thousand other outings in ice country, with new memories born each winter.

Some fishing excursions are memorable for reasons other than the number of fish caught. One of my most enjoyable ice fishing trips came on a Christmas day just a few years ago. I'd worn a tie, of all things, through the biggest part of the holiday morning. Ozzie and Harriet would have been proud, I was being so respectable. I even tried not to look longingly outdoors as the mercury in the thermometer pushed up to a relatively balmy 30 degrees. Mary Jo, bless her, finally leaned over and whispered into my ear — "Let's go ice fishing."

In ten minutes I'd traded the tie and dress shoes for a wool scarf and felt-pac boots. The car already held my fishing tackle, as it seems to do all winter. We were quickly bound for a warmwater impoundment nearby.

The lake was all-but-deserted, most of its frequent anglers no doubt held ashore by domestic matters and perhaps spouses less understanding than mine.

When a kid with a brand-new pair of Christmas ice skates bladed over to check our progress, he found us with a baker's dozen mix of crappies and bluegills, plus a 25-inch pike we were about to release. We just wanted a few panfish for dinner and a few hours alone in the outdoors. We'd succeeded admirably on both counts.

For either peace or productive fishing, I'll take ice-time, anytime. Usually I find both.

I firmly believe that I catch more fish per hour of effort while ice fishing than in open water. Most ice fishermen with whom I've compared notes agree. There are many reasons offered for the better success rate of ice fishermen, most of them untested.

I think we just do a better job of fishing when the weather's cold and the water's hard. You can always doze off in a boat gently bobbing on a summer lake. A cold drink or a tanned bathing beauty can distract you easily. But in the winter all of nature's forces direct your attention to your fishing line.

A non-fisherman may casually enjoy a June day spent perch fishing, but he won't likely enjoy fishing the same waters for perch when a foot of ice covers the water. If he does, he's no longer a non-fisherman, he's an ice fisherman.

The top of a frozen lake is flat and, unless you've been fortunate enough to have walked onto some clear, black ice through which you can often see bottom and occasionally even a fish or two, it's pretty monotonous.

The only break in the shoreline-to-shoreline ice cover may be the hole you've just cut. And on that hole you focus all your attention. Ice fishing is a darned good reason to be on the ice; and there aren't that many other good reasons.

The colder it gets, the harder you stare at that fishing hole and the line you've threaded down through it. And the more attention you pay to your fishing — in any season — the more success you can expect.

Fish are a bit more predictable in winter than in warm-weather months, too. Perhaps it's because they aren't as active. They are cold-blooded creatures, so when the water temperature drops, so does their metabolism or body activity. They don't burn up as much energy so they don't need to eat as much. But there isn't as much natural food available to them as in summer, either. The major food-producing segment of the lake is closed for the winter. Your offering faces less competition. And since weed growth slumps in winter, the fish can even see your bait more easily.

In summer regular changes in the weather, lake-top activity or other factors can make it impossible to enjoy similar fishing success on two consecutive days. But in winter, if you caught fish from a certain hole in the ice on a certain bait yesterday, you'd best copy your tactics today.

Finally, fish don't seem quite as spooky under the ice as

they do when those same waters are open. The impact of sunlight is reduced when that light is filtered through several inches of ice and snow.

That ice and snow probably cuts the noise, too. Even though snowmobiles rumbling by may disrupt your fishing momentarily, it's still a smaller problem than a summer lake chock-full of ski boats.

The fish you catch in winter will likely taste better than those you caught from the same lake last summer. Mine do, anyway. Maybe it's because of the extra effort involved in catching them through the ice. Or perhaps there's some biological reason involving changes in the fish's diet or activity level.

More likely the superb taste of winter fish results from the cold water, cold air and snow that, together, keep spoilage to a minimum. Experts say a fish begins to deteriorate as soon as it dies. Cold, however, slows that spoilage greatly.

The lake trout you caught at the beginning of this chapter will convince you of the fine eating qualities of ice-caught fish, I'm certain. Keep it cold and fillet it out as soon as you get home.

Cut the orange-ish strips of meat into thin slices, then roll them in whatever batter is handy, even simple pancake flour, and pop the strips into hot oil for a few minutes on each side.

Those chunks of gourmet eating will make strong arguments for a long ice-fishing career. Their taste challenges, but never overshadows, the magic of walking upon frozen water, the mystery of catching big fish far below you, and the charm of hours spent with kindred souls.

We have a lot in common, after all. Even though you're new to the ice and we spend much of the winter upon it, we all jumped with the same alarm when the ice boomed.

It was just more safe ice forming, though, not the surrender of too-thin ice to too-heavy anglers.

We've shared the launching of a winter day. Winter clouds seem so much more powerful than those of summer. They billow higher, roll faster and paint with far more authority the earth beneath them.

When the waters freeze we share domain over every lake. We don't need boats or fancy gear — just an access point from which we can walk onto the frozen waters.

Come again to this lake, or to any of thousands that freeze across the northern United States and Canada each winter. You'll get cold, tired and, once in awhile, maybe even a little bit bored. But when that little bobber dips or the tip-up flag flies, your heart will beat with renewed vigor.

And after a season or two, your spirits will rise nearly as high just remembering a good ice fishing day. You'll look forward to winter when, heavily clothed and in the company of some good friends, you'll savor another ice fisherman's sunrise.

Figure 2 — Divers extract a snowmobile from a lake in which it plunged. The snowmobile dropped through thin ice over a channel between two lakes; the machine's passenger died.

Chapter 2

Safety

STAY DRY & ALIVE

Many times I've chatted with veteran ice anglers, comparing notes on catches, baits and the weather. Then, inevitably, the conversation turns to dunkings, the times they've dropped through the ice, emerging soaked-through but obviously quite alive, their interest in ice fishing undampened.

Maybe they were walking over water only a few feet deep. Perhaps the water was deeper but they were able to use a spud, a knife or a rope thrown by a quick-thinking buddy to pull themselves out. Maybe they were just plain lucky and bobbed back to the surface, kicked their feet, and were out.

The next day, or maybe even yet the same day, they were back on the ice, a little more cautious but no less enthusiastic about their sport.

I know of other anglers, however, who also fell through the ice. They just barely got themselves out, and quickly swore they'd never again trust a frozen body of water to support them.

I know one person who, some 30 years later, still can't

stand to walk upon a skating rink, even though he knows there's concrete, not water, beneath its ice.

Even those folks, however, are among the lucky ones.

During one recent winter in my home state of Michigan, an even dozen people plunged through the ice. Not all were fishermen. Some were on snowmobiles, either for fishing transporation or recreation on its own merits. A few others were traversing frozen lakes or streams in cars or trucks.

The dozen, however they came to be on the ice, had one thing in common. They died. Divers had to pull their bodies from lakes upon which they should have had fun. Their families and friends became survivors, bereaved, when they should have shared many more years with those who drowned.

I was visiting a lake one Saturday morning in February when I noticed a crowd at one end of the lake. Naturally, I went over, camera in hand, to investigate. What I saw saddened, sickened and scared me. Divers from the local sheriff department were clamping heavy cables onto a submerged snowmobile while a wrecker crew stood ready to drag the sled ashore. Nobody seemed anxious to talk about what had happened to the snowmobile's riders.

Later I found that a husband and wife had been on this machine the previous night. New to the lake, they didn't know that it was connected by an open channel to another small lake, and into that channel they had driven.

A quick-thinking bystander had rescued the driver of the machine; his wife was pulled from the water 40 minutes later and was rushed to a hospital.

She lay in that hospital while the snowmobile was pulled from the icy waters. She lay there for several days before she died.

That same weekend, elsewhere in the state, an ice fisherman died when the pick-up truck he was driving plunged through the ice over a Great Lakes Bay.

These stories are all too familiar to any newspaper reader in ice country. Every year people die after falling through ice. In almost every case, one or more violations of basic safety precautions can be pinpointed as the cause of the tragedy.

The rules of ice safety are in some ways like the rules for safe operation of an automobile. You can bend the rules, or break them outright, and get away with it — sometimes. But no matter how often or how seldom you break the rules, there's a chance that when you do, you're going to get caught. On ice, like in a car, you just might pay for breaking the rules with your life.

The first rule of ice safety is respect. Ice is not a living creature, of course, but it often resembles one. It's born, gaining strength through its early life. Occasional illnesses may reduce its strengh. Eventually, it's going to weaken and finally, it's going to pass away. You simply have to respect the ice, always keeping an eye alert for changes, indications that it's unsafe. And temper every decision with the knowledge that the water beneath it can easily and quickly take your life.

You must be responsible for your own actions. We're living in an age when its increasingly fashionable to find someone else to shoulder our blame for us. Stub your toe on a sidewalk and sue the owner or the sidewalk maker. Never mind that you didn't watch for the obstacle or lift your foot above it. Maybe that mind-set works in a court of law, but not on the ice.

Whether or not you choose to ice fish or pursue another sport on a frozen lake is your decision, and it's a very personal one. Once made, it's you who must guard your own safety.

There have been many basic rules listed through the years on just what constitutes safe ice. These list ice thicknesses in inches, matching those measurements to activities which are considered safe. They're good guidelines, generally, but that's all. There are too many other variables that directly and emphatically affect ice safety.

Eric Olsen is a marine education specialist for the Michigan Department of Natural Resources. Much of the year that means he's an ice-safety specialist. Having spent countless hours on the ice for both work and recreation, he has the expertise.

Olsen described for me the problems of setting firm ice-safety rules. "It is impossible to make a comment on what is safe ice and have it cover all situations. While three inches of ice on a farm pond may hold a person with little danger, that same three inches on a moving stream or (on) a lake with springs, stumps, marine growth and currents, could be very dangerous. On the Great Lakes, one step from three-foot ice you may find a lead with nothing more than skim ice and a little snow." The cause is sub-bodies of water that freeze at different rates.

Conditions vary, and it's your job to keep track of them. The first piece of ice fishing equipment I recommend is a spud, a tool that most resembles a long-handled chisel. Store salesclerks tell you spuds are for chipping holes in the ice, and they do work well for that. But they've a far more important role as tools to test the thickness of the ice.

Whenever there's the least shadow of a doubt about the thickness of a lake's ice — and that's most of the time — I walk very slowly onto the ice, thudding the ice soundly with a heavy spud on each step or two. More than once my jaw has dropped when a good tap poked right through the ice. That obviously meant there was far too little ice for me to be walking upon, and I quickly backpeddled to shore to wait for another batch of cold weather to firm up the footing.

(This isn't exactly a safety matter, but make sure your spud has a wrist strap so that when testing ice or spudding a hole, you can't let the spud slip through your hands when the last thud pokes through the ice. Many spuds lie at lake bottom, unable to perform the safety and hole-cutting jobs for which they were designed.)

Tunking the ice with each step is the first job of the spud. The second is to chop test holes. I like being able to kneel down, look at the ice — maybe even measure it with my hands — and know for certain just how thick and safe it is.

But don't, please, chop test holes right in the path on which other anglers will walk.

My only ice-fishing dunking came one day when I took

my wife to a popular fishing spot from which I had been taking bluegills and crappies for several weeks.

I knew the ice was about six inches thick. As I had many days before, I stepped off the end of a dock at water's edge — only this time I kept right on going, clear up to my waist. Now wide awake, I turned to see the half-angry, half-amused face of my wife. "How can I help you?" she asked, and I mumbled something ambiguous as I pulled myself back onto the dock.

The fishing trip — along with my comfort and composure — was shot, just because someone had decided to chop their test hole at the end of the dock and because I'd been too excited about fishing to look carefully at the ice there.

Remember always that ice quality varies greatly, from lake to lake, season to season, even day to day. It can be the good clear blue or black ice that signals strength, or it can look porous, milky, spongy, rotten or honey-combed. Stay on shore unless certain the ice is safe.

And don't ever assume that an entire lake is covered with the same quality or thickness of ice. While researching this book I cut a hole in the ice of a lake near home. It was about 10 inches thick. A little later, after a half-hour fishing session that brought no action, I moved about 50 yards away to try a different hole. I was shocked to find the ice there just three inches thick. That didn't spook me off the ice, since that was enough for my walk-on fishing. But to a snowmobiler or, God forbid, an on-ice car driver, it could have meant disaster.

Variations in ice are especially common along shore, where ice is often thinnest to start with and the quickest to deteriorate when water levels change, sun starts the melt-down process, or run-off waten begins cutting it. Deadheads, docks, posts and stream inlets and outlets spell trouble, too. Moving water and warmth cut ice. Objects that, being dark, draw the heat of sunlight create a danger zone.

And if you're going to fish on the impounded lake waters of a river, be especially careful. Current, always remember, cuts ice.

Two situations make ice-checking even more important. The season's first ice is often inconsistent. And if the ice forms a little, then is covered with a few inches of snow, the white blanket has an insulating effect, keeping the ice from quickly building up a safe thickness.

Spring-fed lakes are especially tricky, too. Often they'll have patches of thin ice all winter.

Here are some more general rules: new ice is generally much stronger than old ice; a couple of inches of new, clear ice may be strong enough to support you while even a foot or more of old, air-bubbled ice may not.

Now, for the thickness guide, which we have already said just starts the job of determining whether your favorite lake is safe for fishing. These are the minimums as suggested by the Michigan DNR; your standards should be at least this conservative.

Stay off ice that's only one-inch thick. On two-inch ice, you may be able to fish on foot and in widely-scattered groups. Your group can fish, still separately, with a little more ease on three-inch ice, and on four inches of the hard stuff you can finally start to relax and enjoy your fishing. Don't snowmobile on any ice less than five inches thick.

(I think a lot of snowmobilers get into trouble, too, because it's so easy to travel long distances over the ice without checking or even considering changes in ice thickness between point A and point B.)

How much ice does it take to make driving an automobile upon it safe? That's a good question. People drive cars and trucks on ice every winter, and most of them never experience a problem. But as far as I am concerned the only lake safe for car or truck travel is one frozen completely to the bottom.

If you must drive on the ice, at least keep the windows down and the doors ajar. If your car breaks through and the windows and doors are tight, there'll be too much water pressure against them for you to get out of the vehicle. And be ready always to bail out of the car in case of trouble. Seat belts are great when you're driving on a road; keep them unbuckled, though, when on the ice, since they'd make escape just that much slower.

No matter how I'm moving across the ice — whether on foot, on a snowmobile or in a car — I try to tell myself two things every time I go ice fishing: (1) sooner or later, I'm going to break through, and (2) by exercising caution, I can substantially lessen the odds that it's going to happen on this particular day.

Think ahead. Realize that you can indeed break through. Olsen urges ice anglers to wear a personal flotation device (life jacket) and I think that's darned good advice. The new foam-type vests are even comfortable and good insulation against the cold.

Here are some other ice safety tips Olsen passed along, for that day when you eventually plunge through the ice:

"If you do go through the ice stay on top of the water. Don't let yourself be pulled down by your snowmobile. Remember, your clothes will help you float for awhile."

"Get out any way you can," Olson continued. "If you can, get your upper body up on the ice and use whatever handholds you can to roll out of the water. Stay spread out and squirm, crawl or roll to safety. You may have to float on your back and work your way out by kicking your feet and actually swimming out of danger. The decision must be made fast and your decision executed just as fast. It won't be long before you start feeling the ill effects of hypothermia. When you get out and are on safe ice, get to warmth and safety as quick as possible. If you are alone and headed for a car, get your car keys out as soon as you leave the water. That may be impossible in a minute or two, after your pockets freeze solid."

In most cases the path you took to the hole is the safest one away from it. Roll away from the hole until you can safely stand up. Your clothes will quickly freeze, so get moving toward safety.

Maybe you're not the one who went through, but some-one near you has. What do you do? Said Olsen, "If you are assisting someone from the ice, do not place yourself in the same jeopardy. You will do them no good if you both go through. Use a ladder, tree limb, article of clothing, rope or anything else you can lay your hands on to assist them. If you have to go on the ice, spread your weight as much as possible. If you have a line and the person in the water is still able, have them tie it around them. In a very few minutes their hands will be too cold to hold on."

Olsen added that often a person rescued from the ice may seem beyond help — dead. But new medical procedures, and a phenomenon known as the "mammalian diving reflex" make it possible that the person can be saved. If you have been trained in cardiopulmonary resuscitation (and all outdoor folks should be; contact your local American Red Cross), use it to preserve the possibility of life and get the person to a hospital.

None of that sounds like much fun, does it? Even though these tips could easily save a life, it's so much better to use the respect and judgment required to avoid such emergencies.

Whatever you do, don't trust someone else's judgment. I sat on a large lake one day, on good ice between two and three inches thick. Just about the minimum for widely-scattered anglers. I fished awhile, looked up, and watched a snowmobile zooming across that lake, several hundred yards further out from shore. I know that had he stopped his machine, or had it stalled, the machine and driver would have plunged through the ice.

And I'm not even sure that the ice would have been thick enough to allow me to go to his rescue. Since that startling sight I've never rushed onto a fishing spot just because others were already there.

I'd rather be the foolish-looking angler who carefully taps the ice with a spud, sneaking so cautiously onto the ice, only to find with the first test hole that there's a solid 18 inches of ice. Play it safe, then laugh at how safe you're playing it.

It's my butt that gets wet, or my life that ends, if I don't play it safe and I fall through. So it's my job to make sure it doesn't happen. Safety only requires a few minutes of any trip, leaving you free to relax and enjoy the remainder of the outing. Ice, properly respected, is a platform on which you can build many enjoyable fishing experiences.

Figure 3 — Dressed properly an ice fisherman can remain comfortable even on a stormy winter day. This angler's hood and windproof outer coat allow him to ignore the wind at his back — and concentrate on bluegills on a snowy day.

Chapter 3

Stay Warm

To enjoy ice fishing you must first learn to respect ice and minimize the chances of a fall through it. We covered that in the preceeding discussion. But nearly as important is your own warmth. If you don't stay warm, you'll become either a miserable ice fisherman or a former ice fisherman. You must be comfortable to pay adequate attention to your fishing, too.

Fortunately, more good cold-weather clothing is now available, at reasonable prices, than ever before. For an ice angler a few decades ago, the choice of cold-weather clothing material was simple: wool. Long underwear, shirt-jackets, outerwear — all were of wool, and for good reason. Wool is an excellent insulator and, especially important to the ice fisherman, wool retains much of its insulating worth when wet. An ice fisherman clad in wool could venture out in practically any weather, even rain or snow, and put in a full fishing day without chill. But wool is heavy when dry and almost unbearably heavy when wet. And it's bulky; walking to your fishing spot might leave you sweat-soaked — still warm, but certainly not comfortable.

The other attire ally of the ice fisherman a decade or two ago was goose down. Down-filled clothing, much of it military surplus, provided good insulation and comparatively light weight. The clothing was still bulky, however, and practically no good at all when wet. I learned that one day by snowshoeing clad in a down-filled coat. I perspired heavily, the coat became soaked, and I darned near froze.

There are still important places for woolen and down-filled clothes in today's ice fishing wardrobe. But synthetic materials are becoming more important and popular each year. We can probably thank the snowmobile for those innovations. When the tracked machines became super-popular in the 1960s and 1970s, the people who were buying power sleds clamored for clothing that would keep them warm.

Responding to that demand the cold-weather clothing industry made available one-piece, synthetic-filled, nylon-shelled jump suits. These suits were wind-resistant, hooded, and built to last. Many of them are still in use today.

And the snowmobile suit is still a good bet for the ice fisherman. Buy one large enough to allow free movement, even with extra heavy clothes underneath it.

I'm a fan of the two-piece suit. I prefer bibbed overalls with a heavy coat over them. The two-piece suit offers many of the advantages of the snowmobile suit, along with the extra flexibility of being able to leave the coat open if the day is warm, close it tightly if it's cold, or remove it entirely if working hard spudding a hole or enjoying an unusually-nice spring-time ice fishing outing. The chest portion of well-made bib overalls is as good as a vest.

Which is the fill for you? That's a tough question. I'd go synthetic, first of all. Modern fills are nearly as warm as dry down, and offer certain decided advantages. Most retain much of their insulating properties if they become wet. (The explanation of that phenomenon is fairly simple. Fill doesn't keep you warm; it's the dead air space within it that does the job. Wet down packs tight, while wet synthetic fills still trap air and keep much of their loft. The result is that you stay relatively warm.) Man-made materials wash up more easily, dry quicker, and are in many cases cheaper than those filled with down.

Several companies manufacture top-quality synthetic fills. Generally, you get what you pay for. Pay the extra up-front for a good suit; you'll be counting on it for years of warm fishing.

A nylon shell is probably best for ice fishermen. It is nearly wind-proof, cleans easily and is often less expensive than a cloth- or blend-type shell. I hedge here myself, though. My own ice fishing suit has a cloth-type shell, camouflage-colored, and it serves double-duty for late-season deer and duck hunting and early-season, open-water fishing. I chose the cloth covering to keep noise to a minimum while bowhunting.

Fabrics are even available now that allow perspiration to escape from the inside while keeping water from soaking through. Gore-Tex brand is the leader here, and all types of outerwear are now made with it.

Almost as important as the suit itself are the items of clothing you wear beneath it. For years backpackers and other winter sports enthusiasts have championed the principle of layering — wearing a larger number of lighter pieces of clothing, so that layers, or items of clothing, can be added or removed to adjust for changing weather conditions and activity levels. The ice fisherman can follow their example with excellent results.

First, the long underwear. This is largely a matter of personal choice. For all but the very coldest of weather, most styles and materials of long johns work well. Even inexpensive cotton long underwear works, but I prefer either woolen long johns when I can find them, (I'm fortunate in that wool doesn't irritate me as it does some others), a wool-cotton blend, or heavier, quilted clothes. Some new materials, such as polypropylene, are good for skiing and other active outdoor sports, but less so for rather stationary ice fishermen.

If you're really serious about staying warm, wear something other than blue jeans over the long john bottoms. Experts say there's little with less insulating value than denim. It gets wet easily, stays clammy long, and doesn't add much warmth. Pull on a pair of corduroy trousers or, better yet, a pair of woolen ones.

On your torso, too, wool is hard to beat. Your suit will protect it from getting wet and heavy from rain or snow, and its good insulating value when damp will protect you from your own perspiration. I wear a turtle-neck wool sweater, topped with a wool shirt, under my suit, and I can fish in temperatures well below zero in relative comfort.

Whatever assortment of clothing you assemble, make sure at least one piece has a heavy hood. You'll almost certainly be wearing a stocking cap or hat with ear flaps, since experts say that much of a person's heat loss is through the head. But when the winds begin to whip across a frozen lake, the hood adds immeasureable comfort atop the hat. And whether or not the hood is on your head, it guards the back of your neck against those cold winds.

When trying on outwerwear you plan to wear ice fishing, make sure it leaves you plenty of room to move. Wear the stuff you think you'll have on underneath, and maybe a little more, and make sure you can still spud a hole, crank an auger, and bend to fight a fish.

Across the ice fishing region, cross-country and downhill skiing are very popular, too. When you're looking at outerwear make sure you don't pick ski-wear just because it is more colorful or fashionable. Skiers are generally more active than ice fishermen, especially cross-country skiers. And downhill skiers are much closer to a warming house. Clothes made for those sports are often far lighter than what you need for ice fishing.

We've left the appendages — hands and feet— to last. That's due partly to my reluctance to tackle those portions of the anatomy, since no two ice fishermen agree upon what's best. The hands are the easier of the two, however. First, forget about gloves. They separate the fingers so the digits can't share their warmth one with the other.

Get mittens instead. You can scrunch your hands around to move warmth back into them and your hands will stay much warmer. There are few ice fishing chores you can accomplish in gloves that can't be done in mittens anyway. You almost have to fight fish and rebait hooks bare-handed. So slip off the mitts, get the job done, and rewarm your hands later. Many ice fishermen also carry liquid- or solid-fuel handwarmers. They're not very expensive, and well worth the cost if the weather's really cold or windy.

Pick mittens that easily cover the cuffs of your coat. A narrow slice of exposed wrist skin can chill your entire body and your enthusiasm for fishing. Make sure you can remove the mitts easily when fishing action really gets going. Beyond that, find a pair that feel good. Some fishermen like oversized snowmobile mitts. Others favor ski mitts with either nylon or leather covers over a filled or fleecy interior. I have leather ones lined with fleece. I treat them each season or two with a good waterproofing paste and have never had them soak through. The same pair of mitts have seen heavy duty for more than five years; obviously, a good pair of mitts is a sound ice fishing investment.

I also tuck a pair of military surplus woolen glove liners into my fishing suit. They're handy just in case I drop a mitt into the ice fishing hole — which I have done — or in case the weather is just too awful to fish bare-handed — which it has been. You can also loan them to a fishing buddy who is nowhere near as well-prepared as yourself. That's fun, too.

A down- or synthetic-fill vest is always good for extra warmth. It can even be rolled tightly into a small package and carried in your equipment bucket or backpack in case weather worsens during the day.

Finally, now, to the feet. If I had plenty of money available and either walked short distances to my fishing spots or traveled to them by snowmobile or car, I'd use only military surplus, Mickey-Mouse-style boots, the kind issued during the Korean War.

That is, of course, provided I could find them. You may be able to find a pair in a surplus store. There are different models designed for protection at different temperatures. Stick with authentic boots; foreign import copies aren't always as good. And remember how heavy they felt when you lifted them in the store; they'll be far heavier on your feet when you trudge across a lake wearing them. But a pair of Mickey Mouse boots over a couple of pairs of heavy socks almost guarantees warm feet.

More practical, for a number of reasons, are felt-pac boots. I like those with rubber bottoms, leather uppers, and good-quality felt inserts. My favorite pair even have Vibram lug soles for surer traction and a little more distance between my feet and the cold ice. Steel-toed boots are critical for those whose jobs offer the possibility of falling objects or other accidents; for the ice fisherman they offer only cold steel wrapped around cold toes. Stay away from them.

Other good boots are nylon snowmobile boots, good-quality insulated rubber boots, or even four-buckle arctics pulled over felt-pacs. That's the old predecessor of our felt-pacs; and if you experiment to match plenty of felt with a good fit, your feet will still be well-served.

Socks are another tough subject. There's no substitute for experience in finding the combination of socks that work best for you. Again, I like wool, and several pairs of them. I carry them along on the drive and put them on when we park; that avoids a build-up of perspiration along the way.

I don't wear my felt-pacs on the drive, either. Others like nylon or cotton socks beneath those of wool. Take a few sample trips in different sock combinations and see what works best for you.

Shelters. Here's probably the most enjoyable example of the ice fisherman's ingenuity. Most of the tarps, tents, lean-tos, wrap-arounds and shanties or coops on any lake are homemade or home-designed. All have good points, and all have just-as-common drawbacks.

If I were in real need of a shelter, it would be a shanty or coop. But first I'd have to know that I'd be fishing on the same general area of a lake through much of the ice season. Regularly chopping a shanty out of the ice and snow doesn't appeal to me. Most states have laws regulating the use of shanties, too, so do some research before you start building one.

Basically, a shanty or coop is a customized version of an old-style outhouse. The holes, however, are in the floor instead of the seat. You sit on the bench. Shanties are critical for spear-fishing, as we'll discuss in a later chapter, and handy as well for tip-up and jigging-rod fishing. When designing your shanty make sure there's room enough for the type of fishing and number of anglers you anticipate will join you, then add some space just to be on the safe side. Make it as wind-proof as possible, but don't forget to provide adequate ventilation so that fumes from whatever heat source you choose can escape. Some shanty fishermen have suffocated from fumes.

Once those basics are covered, the range of shelter possibilities is endless. The subject of shanties could fill an entire book, rather than just part of one chapter. (For a fun look at shanties, see the chapter entitled "Making Do.") You could even build a convincing case on the fishing shanty as an item of American folk craft. For a practical fishing shelter, however, study those on the ice where you fish. Most shanty-builders are more than proud to show off their shelters. Decide how big you want yours, of what material you'll build it, and how you'll equip it. You can add a wood stove or use gasoline lanterns for both heat and light, and build shelves or cabinets for gear. Don't forget to equip it with a good hasp and lock. Even then, you probably should carry your most expensive gear back off the ice at the end of the day. It's a sad fact of life that someone may break in, or break up, your shanty while you're away.

There are, of course, other ways to protect yourself from the elements. I was interested, one cold day on a large, windy lake, when the two locals showing me this fishery chopped three holes in the ice, planted wooden poles in them, repacked the holes with water and slush, then strung between the poles a canvas tarp. With a small fire on the lee side of the canvas, we had both wind protection and heat.

Figure 4 — This wrap-around shelter consists of a canvas windscreen supported by a conduit frame. It folds to fit into the box towed behind a snowmobile.

Other anglers turn a piece of plywood into a portable shelter. They cut the 4x8 sheet into two pieces four feet long by two feet wide. Hinge the two together along their long edges, then frame both sheets along their edges and horizontally about two feet from the base. Two triangular pieces of plywood are then cut to fit over nails in the framing, one at the bottom and the other halfway up, for a seat. This shelter easily folds flat, then unfolds for a corner-shaped shelter. You can add skis or runners to make it easy to pull across the lake, or place a lantern under the seat-board for heat.

Some of the most clever shelters I've seen are wrap-around canvas windscreens erected on sled boxes towed behind snowmobiles. These are fitted to conduit tubing frames so the whole assembly fits into the box of the sled. Once on site you can quickly erect the shelter (some of which even have tops) and fish in comfort, without all the hassles of building, moving and worrying about a large shanty. The other advantage of these shelters is that they're anchored to the snowmobile. Except for the heaviest of shanties, most other shelters are vulnerable to high winds.

Staying warm isn't just a matter of comfort, though. Ice fisherman should be aware of hypothermia, the malady most newspaper accounts call exposure. It is the cooling of the body's core temperature, the warmth of the vital organs. It can lead directly to death.

The first rule regarding hypothermia is not to fish or travel outdoors alone. One of the first symptoms of the onset of the malady is impaired judgment; you may need a clear-thinking partner to come to your aid.

The body is a temperature-maintenance machine. Hypothermia, simply, means that machine can't keep up with the conditions.

Normal body core temperatures, not necessarily the same as those of your extremities, are near the well-known 98.6-degree mark. Below that range hypothermia sets in. Between about 97 and 93 degrees, experts say, shivering begins. Not just a shudder or two, but uncontrollable shivering. Below 93 degrees, shivering stops and your muscles become rigid. That's what paints the classic picture of a hypothermia or exposure victim stumbling through the snow. At about 86 degrees you lose consciousness, risk heart failure, and face dangers that come with the shock of rewarming.

It's difficult (impossible without training) to deal with the advanced stages of hypothermia in remote areas. So make sure you learn to recognize it early.

If chilling occurs because of wet clothing, change it for dry. Water and wind reduce body temperature drastically, so stay dry and conserve heat, whether a hypothermia victim, a potential one, or the companion of one. Emergency blankets made of space-age materials, or even just a big plastic bag, keep wind and water off the hypothermia victim.

Experts say the hypothermia victim often feels the urge to hunker down to conserve heat. That's better than exercise, which just burns up more of the body's energy and heat, already in short supply.

You can help the hypothermia victim with your own body heat, or by immersing his body, but not arms and legs, in warm but not hot water. Make sure, though, that if shivering stops it's a sign of recovery and not deepening of hypothermia. And never give up on a person who appears dead from exposure. Hypothermia mimics death; doctors may still be able to save the victim.[1]

Common sense is the best way to avoid exposure. Dress correctly for the weather. If the conditions are truly miserable, especially if you're wet, call off the outing. Fishing is only fun when you're comfortable, and can be downright dangerous when you're not. Remember how strongly we stressed respecting ice? It's the same way with winter weather; respect it, and your body's temperature maintanance system will do the rest.

[1]The subject of hypothermia from prevention to methods of treatment is thoroughly covered in Hypothermia — Death by *Exposure* by William W. Forgey, M.D., published by ICS Books, Inc. 1985.—ED.

Chapter 4

Panfish

The tiny bobber did little more than quiver. My partner's eyes caught that slight movement, though, and his body tensed, his attention riveted to the six-inch-wide hole in the five-inch-thick ice. He raised the jigging rod just high enough to remove the slack between it and the little float. And when the bobber dipped again he struck, folding the light rod into an arc, then dropping it to the ice as he grabbed the light line.

The fight itself was quick. Only about six feet of line separated the angler from his adversary. Still, my buddy tugged on the fish gingerly, especially as it came closer to the surface. Then he slipped his hand into the water, just far enough to flip onto the ice a seven-inch bluegill.

The fish, brightly-arrayed in blues, greens and yellows, flopped once or twice on the ice, finally coming to rest against a dozen or so of its colleagues. My partner smiled admiringly, rebaited his hook and lowered it again to the bottom.

This scene, real as it was, wouldn't have to be cast with

Figure 5 — An fisherman ices a scrappy bluegill.

my fishing partner as the protagonist. The quarry wouldn't even have to be a bluegill. The casting could just have easily included you, the setting any lake in this country's ice-fishing region, and the fish could have been a bluegill, sunfish, white or black crappie, rock bass or white bass.

I regard all those species as panfish. Perch are panfish, too, but tactics and tackle are enough different for them that a separate chapter follows. All the panfish mentioned above offer a brand of winter fishing that's action-packed, enjoyably simple, and almost universally available.

Many of us launched our fishing careers when we triumphantly landed a panfish, likely from the open waters of a warmwater lake. The saucer-shaped fish, no matter how long nor how short, was a trophy. It's capture darned-near guaranteed that we'd be back for more.

Panfishing can get into your blood just as easily when you catch your first one through the ice. Like its summer counterpart, the ice-caught panfish is a willing feeder; few are the days when a panfisherman on ice gets completely skunked. It's a scrappy battler, too; on light tackle you'll never be sure of defeating a panfish until it's on the ice. And I've seen more than one flop its way across the ice, back into the hole and away to freedom. And the panfish is sure a welcome, tasty contribution to the dinner table; I wouldn't trade the first mess of winter-caught panfish for any other fish dinner, any time of the year.

Panfish are substantially less active in the winter than in summer, but conversely I've seen more periods of non-stop fishing action in the winter than I've ever witnessed in open water.

Here's how you can get in on that action.

Winter panfishing is simple. All you need (and we'll discuss more complicated rigs and tactics in a minute) is an inexpensive, light-weight jigging rod about two feet long, available in any sporting goods store. You can even make one yourself from surviving parts of broken open-water tackle. Reels aren't necessary; clip-on or peg-type line holders are fine. To the rod add a short length of good-quality four-pound test monofilament line, a bobber, small lures and some bait, and you're ready for basic panfishing.

Of all the panfisherman's tackle, I think line is the most important and most-often overlooked. Keep it light. If this chapter makes one point, it should be that winter panfishing requires a more subtle approach.

Here's an admittedly subjective rule for winter panfishing. Never use any monofilament line stronger than four pounds test for panfish. Two-pound test is probably better yet, and I know some serious bluegillers who use nylon sewing thread which tests at one pound or less. But the new fisherman should start with four-pound. It will work on all but the most skittish fish and is far easier to handle than the lighter stuff. Once you're used to this type of fishing, you can lighten up later if fishing conditions demand it.

Why, you might well ask, must one scale down his or her gear so drastically for winter fishing when heavier line, big hooks and large bobbers work on panfish, summer after summer?

The answer is complicated, and actually consists of several answers. First off, I'd bet your summer success, good as it may be, would improve if you used lighter tackle. That said, let's take a little closer look at a winter lake.

Your favorite bluegill or crappie lake is ice-covered and has been that way for several weeks. A blanket of snow covers it, too. Both factors come quickly to bear on the fish within that lake. Lakes get oxygen from two sources — interchange with the air, and the production of oxygen by green plants growing underwater. Remember photosynthesis from that high school biology class? From spring through fall the lake's oxygen levels are recharged by both sources. But when fall stretches into winter, the days shorten, cutting back on the oxygen production of the green plants. Ice covers the lake and even less sunlight reaches the plants. Many die, others become dormant. And the ice that covers the lake effectively seals it off from oxygen in the atmosphere.

When oxygen becomes scarce, fish become less active.

Another change takes place within your favorite lake in

winter, too. The water, naturally, has cooled. Fish are cold-blooded and, like all creatures of that type, match their metabolism (or body activity) to their environment. When the water turns cool, that too makes the fish less active.

So now the bluegill that inhaled a popping bug with such gusto last summer is semi-dormant. He's not moving around as much, and he's not all that hungry. He might pause and snatch a small morsel during his limited tours but not, likely, a big meal. And he's usually not rushing to that dinner, either, except on those rare and delightful occasions when winter panfish seem to go on a feeding binge.

Generally, if you want to catch panfish through the ice, you're going to have to match your tackle and tactics to the fish and its lifestyle; smaller baits, less movement and more delicacy. You're going to have to work harder and be both more patient and more attentive.

A summer bluegill, for example, will submerge a two-inch bobber and keep right on going. But some of the winter's most productive action comes only after the angler has learned to watch for the tiny sign of a strike. Winter panfish don't hit hard, they don't stick around long, and they take a bait quite gently. If you snooze, you lose. Light tackle gives you the best odds of fooling that fish, sensing its strike and enjoying a scrappy, light-action battle. You don't need heavy gear, anyway.

I've caught several 20-inch-and-better northern pike through the ice on my light panfish gear. Every year some big bass are brought atop the ice on light tackle. Ditto for walleyes. We even iced a six-pound carp one winter day when it decided a wax worm threaded onto a tear-drop hook looked good. Winter fish, especially those of the warmwater variety, aren't nearly as apt to bust up your tackle as summer fish.

The above discussion just might sound like a strong case against fishing for panfish in the winter. After all, we've implied that they don't feed well and don't fight well. That's terribly misleading. Despite the metabolic slowdown of the panfish, I'd bet that winter fishing is more productive, hour for hour, than the warmweather version of the sport.

Here are a few reasons why. Just as the lake's oxygen factory has shut down for the winter, the food factory is nearly idle, too. Particularly in early winter and late winter, there's more hunger than food. That's what makes your bait more attractive to the fish and makes your winter angling days so productively enjoyable. You're likely also paying more attention to your fishing than you do in the summer. After all, there's no ball game on the radio, you can't stretch out and catch a suntan, and it's too cold to drink beer. About the only reason to be on a winter lake is to fish — so you concentrate and do a better job.

Initially, let's lump all the panfish together — bluegills, sunfish, white and black crappies, even rock and white bass. The same basic tackle and tactics will take all of them, so let's set up a basic rigging and strategy.

There's nothing necessarily fancy about a panfish rod for the ice fisherman. For a couple of bucks you can buy a jigging rod that will work admirably. Pick one two or three feet long, limber enough to transmit the feel of a strike, rigid enough to ice that fish.

Most commercially-made rods have wooden handles, and I've caught lots of fish with them. If building my own, though (which is a good idea if you have a spinning or fly rod tip left from a warmweather disaster), try a cork handle. I think they're a little better at telegraphing a strike. For the same reason many ice anglers are switching to graphite jigging rods. I have a two-foot jigging rod made of a graphite blank with a cork handle, and I credit it with increasing my catch on days when bites are light.

Jigging rods come with several types of line-holding systems. The simplest consists of a pair of L-shaped hooks, around which the line is wound. Wooden pegs glued into the handle work well, as do clip-on holders. Some ice fishermen like small plastic reels, but I've not yet found them necessary.

BOBBERS

I advise you to start your winter panfishing career by using a bobber. Many veteran anglers swear by spring-steel strike indicators that lay atop the rod and bend gently when there's a strike. They're great most of the time, but windy conditions can make them less effective. I've never had any problems with a bobber, provided it's of the right type.

I use peg-type ice fishing bobbers exclusively. Peg-type bobbers are easy to identify. They're round or nearly so, with a hole drilled through the center through which the fishing line runs. A wooden or plastic peg presses into the hole to secure the line.

Whatever your do, don't use the big red-and-white plastic push-button bobber you used all summer. We've already established that panfish aren't nearly as aggressive in winter as they are in the summer. Most crappies or bluegills won't pull a big bobber underwater if you allow them all day to do it. And they've another interesting trait that rules out the use of these big floats.

I can't count the times that the small, balsa or sponge, peg-type bobber I use for panfish has, instead of standing straight, tipped slightly to one side, or floated completely on its side. When that happens I always set the hook and, more times than not, I've felt the resistance of a fighting fish at the other end. My best guess is that the fish approached the bait from below, gently inhaled it, and remained beneath the bobber. What I know for certain is that there's a negative pull on the bobber. And I know equally well that no push-button bobber would ever have told me about the strike.

Toss a peg-type bobber into a sink filled with water, with no weight beneath it, and it floats on its side. Now toss in an unweighted push-button bobber. It may float in the same position as it sits on the water while fishing, or it may float completely upside down. But it won't slide smoothly to its side to telegraph a strike. Now put the peg-type bobber on your line and the push-button model back in your summer tackle box. The best bobber for ice fishing for panfish is the smallest peg-type float that will hold your bait off bottom. Dime-sized is about the maximum.

LURES

For most panfish you can't go wrong with a tear-drop-shaped lure. Baited with a grub (wax worm, corn borer, mousie or wiggler), or with a minnow, any of a number of tear-drop colors will catch panfish. If limited to a few, I'd pack tear drops in red, bright orange, chartreuse, and white. I'd keep trying different colors until I found what produced the best on that particular day.

To rig up, pick up the jigging rod and wind four-pound test monofilament line onto the pegs, hooks or reel. I like to wrap about four times as much line as the maximum depth I'll be fishing with the rod. That way, if the line gets hopelessly tangled (which it will, sooner or later), or is broken off by a big fish, I need only trim it back, tie on another tear-drop, adjust my bobber and I'm back in business.

Run the line through the bobber, replacing the peg afterwards, and tie on the tear-drop.

WEIGHT

Did you notice that I've not mentioned the use of split-shot on the line? There's good reason. I'll only use split shot when absolutely necessary. There may be times when it's just too windy to feed line into a hole without extra weight. Sometimes active minnows require some weight to keep them in place. But unless absolutely essential, leave the shot off the line. I've fished for panfish in winds of up to 30 miles per hour without adding weight.

The only situations in which I think weight is a good idea is (a) if fishing in waters more than 30 feet deep, or (b) minnow-fishing. In either case I'd still try fishing clean lines first. For remember what we just said about a panfish coming up from beneath a lure, just tipping the bobber? If you have even a small split shot on the line eight inches above the lure, the fish would have to rise that high or more to inform you of the strike.

That's really about all there is to rigging up. To catch panfish through the ice you need only one jigging rod, so-equipped. But again, it's a good idea to keep changing lures throughout the day, until you find the color panfish favor most. You can, of course, snip off the unproductive lure and tie on another, but I'd rather keep my fingers warm for rebaiting hooks and unhooking fish. I'll often walk onto the ice with as many as a half-dozen jigging rods jammed into a five-gallon plastic pail. Our state law allows an angler to fish with only two lines, but there's nothing wrong with having others at the ready. If one tear-drop doesn't produce, I don't change the lure — I change rods. The selection of rods is further insurance against a calamity befalling any one rod, line or lure.

Finally, now, you're ready for the ice, clad in warm clothing, sure of the safety of the ice, laden with a spud or auger and a bucket filled with jigging rods. Where on your chosen lake will you begin fishing?

LOCATING PANFISH

Panfish and panfishermen are both gregarious. Crappies and bluegills form schools and pursue their food-hunting and other activities together. Panfish anglers form clusters atop the ice over productive fishing spots and, provided you're courteous, they probably won't mind your joining them.

That makes the first part of your fishing trip a little easier. If your lake, like most, boasts a few tight clusters of fishermen, start near one of them. Chances are good the fishrmen are assembled there because the fish are, too.

My standard procedure when approaching a group of anglers is to first mentally compute the distance they've allowed between each other. Then I make sure I don't drill a hole closer than that distance from any one of them. That automatically places you on the outside of the gathering, which is often an advantage. And provided you drill your holes as quickly and quietly as possible, don't let your kids or dog harass the others or play a radio, your angling neighbors are likely to flash you a smile instead of a glare.

Generally, look for panfish to cluster wherever the bottom changes or some structure offers them protection. Drop-offs, especially those that fall from head-high water into depths of 10 to 20 feet, are always good bets. So are sunken brush piles, areas in impounded lakes in which logs lie on bottom, weed bed edges or, especially in mid-winter, deeper holes in the lake.

On my own favorite panfish lake we start the season on first ice less than 15 yards from shore, where the bottom sharply drops to about 12 feet of water. Crappies and blue-gills mix about evenly in the catch. But after a couple of weeks the action and our attention moves several hundred yards offshore. Bluegill action tapers off as we fish 25-foot depths, but the crappies more than make up for it. This is an impounded river backwaters, and before it was flooded decades ago roadbuilders scooped gravel out of this area, leaving a hole that attracts late-winter crappies. But you really wouldn't have to know all that background to find this spot and catch fish from it; there are always a dozen or more fish shanties clustered tightly over the spot, with several dozen anglers toiling outside them.

Suppose I didn't see any groups of anglers on a lake I was to fish, didn't know the lake, and didn't have a map showing its contour. This would be my strategy. I'd start near shore, giving panfish 10 or 15 minutes to go for a certain color of tear-drop baited with a grub, then switching lures for a comparable period of time. I'd try to talk a partner into trying the same spot with different-shaded lures. If our efforts produced no action I'd move, and keep moving until I located fish. The moving activity helps in several ways. Besides helping to locate fish, it takes the chill off you and keeps your interest keen. Usually I'll start fishing in any water four feet deep or deeper, and I'll keep trying until I've tested waters of up to 30 feet.

And if all that didn't work, I'll try a different portion of the lake, a different lake or a different pursuit — for that day, anyway. There are times when all the fish in a specific lake seem to acquire lockjaw at the same time.

But before you give up on the hole, lake area, lake or day, make sure that you're testing each correctly. With very few exceptions, the bulk of your panfish catch will come from near the bottom, usually within a foot of it. So make sure you're fishing in that zone. If fishing line is the most-neglected item of ice fishing gear, which I maintain it is, I'd rate the depth-finding weight as number two. These are cheap to buy and simple to use, yet far too many fishermen don't bother. Often, they're robbing themselves of good fishing. The commercial version of the ice fisherman's depth-finding weight is an electrical-type alligator clip with a hunk of lead molded to it. You can buy them, make your own, or make do with a bell sinker.

Begin checking the depth by removing the peg from your ice-fishing bobber. Then clip the weight to your unbaited lure and unwind enough line to lower the lure and weight to the bottom. Slack line tells you you're on bottom. With the peg removed, the line will feed freely through the bobber and it will continue to float on the surface. When your lure is on bottom, slowly retrieve line until it's just snug, then grasp it firmly in one hand, lifting line and bobber together so they remain in the same spot.

Now you can pull line through the bobber equal to the distance from bottom you want to fish. If you think the fish are eight inches off bottom, pull that much line through the float and replace the peg. Your bobber will hold your lure and bait exactly that far off bottom, each time you remove a fish and return the offering to the productive zone.

Depth-finders do have a habit of turning up missing. I've forgotten them, dropped them in snow too deep to recover them, and once even had a northern pike snip off lure and weight cleanly as I sought bottom. ("How deep is it here," I asked my buddy, who'd fished that spot often. "About five feet," he answered. "Then why haven't I touched bottom with 15 feet of line out?" I countered. The answer was obvious when the line snugged up, a denizen on the other end pulled twice sharply, and I retrieved the line, minus the lure and depth-finder.) Now I carry two or three depth-finders, clipped to pockets, tackle buckets or tucked into pockets, just to make sure there's always one ready. They're that critical to panfish success.

You can, of course, use a portable depth sounder to mark the bottom for you. Most work fine provided you set the transducer in a minnow bucket, puddle of vegetable oil, or the hole you've drilled in the ice. I like to use one for scouting the deeper water haunts for trout, or to locate panfishing cover such as drop-offs and brush piles. But I still rely on the little, cheap depth-finding weights for putting my bait near bottom.

BAITING UP FOR PANFISH

With your bobber set, you're ready to fish. Bait the teardrop with either a grub or minnow. Either will work for panfish on most lakes and, of the two, I prefer grub baits for a couple of rather flimsy reasons. Fish don't steal them as easily, and you don't need to get your hands wet to rebait. Often I'll carry a bucket containing a couple dozen 1 1/2-to 2-inch minnows, just in case the panfish have a decided preference for them. But usually the grubs work, provided they're properly presented on the hook.

Slide the grub onto the hook but don't push it past the point. If the tip of the point shows, you'll cut your action at least by half. It sounds crazy, and I freely admit that I can't guess why a shiny lure attracts fish but a shiny hook point puts them off. But we've tried it both ways, time after time, and I'll stand by my estimate of a 50-percent drop in bites if the hook point shows. It may be even higher.

All types of grubs will work, and my experience finds them working about equally well on panfish. Wax worms, mousies, corn borers, acorn worms, goldenrod grubs — all are good. Whatever your local bait store offers, or whatever you can gather on your own, will probably do the trick just fine.

If fishing with minnows it's best to hook the minnow just under the dorsal fin, although some panfishermen report good results hooking small minnows through the head. Small minnows die quickly, so the jigging action you give the lure is often as important as the natural action of the baitfish.

Lower the bait, carefully watching the line as you do. Sometimes we've found fish suspended off bottom, just by noting slack forming in the line as it's being lowered. Any time the line acts funny, set the hook, just to be sure. And if you hook a suspended fish, slide the bobber further down on the line to continue working that productive range.

If the line feeds freely downward until the bobber is in the water, begin a gentle jigging motion, keeping the lure moving much of the time. I usually lift the rod tip a couple of inches, several times in a row, then let the bobber return to the water. Occasionally I raise the bait a couple of feet, letting the lure flutter back down. And I'm always watching. If the line or bobber acts the least bit unusual — especially if fishing with one of the grub-type baits — I set the hook. Remember the words about bobbers earlier in this chapter? If the float lays on its side it's probably because a fish has nailed the bait on the way down. Sometimes, too, I've watched the bobber hit the water and keep right on going, and quickly I felt the fight of a fish. There are yet other times when you only know a fish is present because the bobber quakes slightly, or moves to one side of the hole, or just because you seem to be developing ice-fishing ESP. But if you think you're having a bite while panfishing, you probably are.

If minnow-fishing for crappies you may have to experiment with the timing of your hook-setting. On some days they can be struck instantly. But on other days, setting the hook before the bobber has gone well underwater will result only in a lost fish.

PANFISH FIGHTING

So now you have a fish on. What to do? After all, you don't have a reel with which to fight the fish. Just a jigging rod, light line and your bare hands. What you do, actually, depends upon where you're fishing.

If the water is less than eight or ten feet deep, I quickly lift the hand with which I'm holding the rod, then grab the line near the ice with my other hand. Then I drop the rod tip, hooking it under the line below my hand-hold, and lift it high again, bringing with it the line. The procedure is repeated wntil the fish is out of the water.

That method works well as long as the line is short enough that you don't form many loops. Otherwise it will quickly become tangled or even knotted on the ice.

When fishing in deeper waters you're better off to set the hook with the rod, lifting it high as before and grabbing the line — then dropping the rod to the ice. Hopefully you've set yourself up with the wind at your back (for your comfort as well as fishing ease) because the wind will carry the line away from the hole as you're retrieving it, keeping it from tangling. I usually hold my left hand close to the ice, pulling line through it with my right hand. When one pull ends, the left hand again holds the line tight. That keeps the link between you and the fish as direct as possible, reducing slack line and, as much as possible, the odds of the fish getting away.

Your set-up will determine how easily you resume your fishing. Hopefully the spud or auger is behind you, where it can't cut or snag your line. And hopefully, too, you cleared the area around the hole of shards of ice or slush left from cutting the hole. They quickly freeze solid and present dozens of obstacles to your smoothly feeding line back down the hole. (That's another reason we suggested starting with four-pound test line; the lighter stuff seems even more prone to fouling on the ice.)

Tangles will occur, so don't despair. If you spy a knot in your line, take the time to cut the line above it and retie the lure. Even a medium-sized panfish and your best lure can be lost if the line breaks at the knot when you set the hook.

Just do whatever you must to get back into action, to get the lure and bait back down to where you now know the fish are located. When you've caught one winter panfish, the odds are great that there are plenty more available right beneath you.

THERE'S A DIFFERENCE

THE GENERAL METHODS described in this chapter will connect you with winter panfish of all species. But there are subtle differences between them and, if you know that one species inhabits a favorite lake, you might want to tailor your tackle and tactics slightly to suit them.

Bluegills

Bluegills are probably the all-time favorite catch of the ice fisherman. Generally, you'll find 'gills in waters slightly shallower than those preferred by crappies. And while bluegills (and closely related sunfish) will on occasion take minnows, grubs of all types are easily the preferred bait.

I know some anglers who fish grubs on plain gold single hooks rather than tear-drop lures, and they report good luck. Others go with tiny Art Best's Russian Hooks, especially in silver and pearl. Ice flies are also good for bluegills.

It's for bluegills that serious anglers most often lighten up their line, sometimes using sewing thread. And since winter bluegills are among the most notorious of light-strikers, it's for them that spring-steel strike indicators are used especially often.

Figure 6 — Bluegills this size are guaranteed to warm the blood of the coldest ice fisherman.

I know one angler, too, who uses a straight line — no rod or bobber — for bluegills, and he claims to enjoy a more direct feel of the subtle strike.

As a general rule the biggest bluegills are found nearer bottom than smaller ones. So if you're catching puny blue-gills, try fishing a little deeper. Bluegills are extremely pro-lific, and in some lakes they become too numerous for proper growth. Such a stunted population can produce fast action on small bluegills, and an angler need feel no shame in keeping a mess. Filleting them can be time-consuming but the exquisite taste is worth it. Quite frankly, there's no tastier catch through the ice than a bluegill.

Anglers who try for bluegills from shanties, from which fish below can often be observed, report that 'gills often inhale a bait and almost instantly spit it out; make sure you're watching your line and bobber all the time, if you want to ice some.

The start-at-bottom rule applies to bluegills, especially early in the season. But as winter deepens the fish seem to move to deeper water and suspend higher above bottom. I once spent far too long fishing near bottom in 30 feet of water in a cluster of anglers. Several of my neighbors were catching fish, one-after-another, and I was fishless. Finally I drew some information out of one of them. "They're about three arm-lengths down," he said. I figured that to be about 15 feet deep and, after I'd moved my lure to that range, I started connecting, too. So don't give up on a bluegill hole, especially in midwinter, until you've tried different depths from the bottom, half-way up.

My best bluegill fishing has come in daylight hours, although some anglers report good luck fishing for them by lantern-light.

Crappies

Crappies come in two brands, white and black crappies. Which you catch depends mainly upon the type of lake in which you're fishing. Throughout much of their collective range, the two species often live in close proximity, some-times even in the same area of one lake. Even though the two are distinct species, and fairly easy to distinguish, most anglers don't bother. For your information, black crappies favor water that is quite clear and which supports plenty of vegetation. Brushy underwater areas seem to produce white crappies, especially if the water is murkier. That's probably why they've done so well in lakes built of dammed river water.

Both species depend heavily upon fish life in their diets, although they're more than happy to inhale a wax worm offered through the ice. I do most of my ice fishing for crap-pies with wax worms, but have seen more than one day when minnows really did the trick. Crappies are also eager feeders at night. Consider spending part of a still winter night on your favorite crappie lake, either in the open or in a shanty. A gas lantern will provide plenty of light and chances are good crappies will provide plenty of action.

Figure 7 — The author admires an ice-caught crappie.

The crappie is known in many areas as old "paper-mouth," for the thin membrane connected to its jaws. That membrane will tear easily if you apply too much force to your line. So be cautious when landing one, especially if it feels like a dandy.

Many anglers bad-mouth the taste of crappies, especially those caught in the summer. I've never objected to the taste of a crappie caught in any season and I've never heard others complain about those extracted from the cold water under a frozen lake top.

Other Species

Other species will probably figure into your catch. We've iced white bass and I've talked to others who mixed rock bass into their bluegill or crappie catch.

Perch — to be covered in a later chapter — are also prized by the panfisherman.

White bass, when you can locate them, take wax worms and minnows well, and provide an exciting under-ice fight.

If I were trying for rock bass I think I'd look for a source of worms.

But any panfish species I know will take grubs or minnows fished the same as you would for crappies or bluegills. Just work on your basic techniques and the bonus species will come your way — and the abundant panfish will provide plenty of action.

Figure 8 — Author's wife, Mary Jo, smiles as she tries for another icewater perch.

Chapter 5

Perch

A SPECIAL PANFISH CASE

If fish could smile, perch would grin. The perch is the angler's friend, and a special pal to the ice fisherman.

Year-around, the perch leads many a state's list of most-often-caught fish. It likewise stands near the top of most lists of the tastiest freshwater fish.

I've caught perch in waters as shallow as two feet, through ice nearly that thick. I've also caught them from waters about 75 feet, while fishing for a deepwater trout. One of my biggest came atop the ice courtesy of a tip-up set for walleyes. Perch just seem to swim everywhere. And every perch, whether from water deep or shallow and whether my fishing target or an unexpected bonus catch, is a welcome addition to my ice-fishing pail. There's little — with the possible exception of the perch's cousin, the walleye — that will rival it on the table.

And while walleyes and other species are known for moodiness, wariness or just plain scarceness, the perch emerges as the angler's friend.

53

Perch can be delightfully simple to catch. Often you need only crude tackle and a rough knowledge of fishing to collect a large bucket filled with perch. But to keep us all humble, there are also times when even the fanciest trick of the most knowledgable perch angler fails to produce fish. Most days will offer challenges somewhere between those two extremes.

In another chapter we describe the commercial development of the Russian Hook perch-fishing lure by Art Best of Sebewaing, Michigan.

Why, the unitiated might ask, would one place such importance on one lure for perch fishing? The answer, in part, is that I feel lucky to have met Art Best and learn some perch-fishing pointers under the tutelage of this late master. The other part of the reason is that the perch is arguably one of the best-eating, most-popular, most cooperative and most widely-distributed fish available to the ice angler.

A closer look at the natural history of perch can pay off in some good fishing tips.

The perch begins life as one egg in a mass of as many as 50,000, deposited on weeds or brush by the female and fertilized by one or more males nearby. That's the last contact a perch has with its parents. The young are left to fend for themselves, and they find the world a hostile place. Up to one-half of the fertilized eggs will hatch within a couple of weeks. And for most of the rest of their lives each of them will be in almost constant demand as dinner, and not just by human anglers.

Walleyes, pike and other perch devour large numbers of small perch. The perch fry, in turn, feed on small zooplankton and insect larvae.

Perch grow quite slowly, reaching two to four inches in their first year of life. At least the one in about 5,000 that survives that first year will reach that length. At two years of age most perch will measure about six inches long, adding about one more inch each year thereafter. But each year, scientists estimate, at least half of the population will be lost to mortality of all kinds.

You'd think that with the long odds facing a perch, they'd be in short supply in most lakes. Actually, the opposite is often the case. Perch tend to overpopulate in many lakes, and that throws a curve into the growth rates described above. Like the goldfish in the bowl in your living room, perch grow only as large as their environment allows. Put too many perch in a lake, and you end up with a stunted population — a lot of perch of all ages, but of short lengths. Bluegills and crappies, incidentally, exhibit the same tendencies. And seldom can sport fishing alone remove enough perch to make a real impact, according to biologists, who sometimes are forced even to poison a lake to remove the numerous, too-small perch and allow a more-balanced ecosystem to rebuild.

Most anglers start keeping perch when they've reached a length of about seven inches. That's when they become noticeably plumper, and when filleting yields at least a three-bite slab of meat.

(That's how I prefer all my panfish, by the way — filleted. My enjoyment of a fish meal is inversely proportional to the number of bones with which I must contend.)

So fishermen like seven-inchers and up. But in most states and provinces there's no minimum length for keeping perch, and I've eaten more than a few yellow perch that were shorter than seven inches. Cleaning small perch can be a chore, but eating them is still a pleasure. And on some lakes you may fish a long time before icing a meal-sized mess of eight-inchers.

LOCATING PERCH

Here's another natural characteristic of perch that will affect your every fishing trip. They begin life in schools of similar-sized fish, and they remain a schooling species throughout their lives. That's both good and bad news for the ice fisherman. You may have to drill many holes before cutting a hole directly above a school of nice-sized perch. But once you've located that school you can enjoy some fast action as long as they remain in the area.

Perch, like walleyes, generally hang close to bottom. Most perch action comes within a foot or so of bottom, regardless of the water depth. Keep your lures within that range.

A multitude of lures and baits are used to catch winter perch. Adult perch consume small fish (including other perch), insect larvae and insects, small crayfish, zooplankton and even snails. And they'll even inhale baits that don't even remotely resemble items in that variety-filled diet.

Perch are a mobile species, forming schools and roaming a lake in search of food. Fall and spring find them in generally-shallower portions of a lake. In midwinter, look for them in shallow areas early and late in the day and in deeper pockets in between — haunts similar to those favored by their cousins, the walleyes. That's just the general rule, however — on any given day you will likely have to prospect, drilling many holes to first find and then keep up with moving perch action.

Unlike walleyes, perch seem to hit best at midday, and sun doesn't seem to bother them. That endears them to anglers who like to sleep in and icefish during the warmest part of the day.

The hardest thing about perch fishing, actually, is doing the legwork required to locate the day's best action. Perch, again, are almost always on the move. So too must you be. If a hole produces no action in a half-hour, you'd best be moving. You may catch fish from the first hole drilled or not until the 25th. But the action will be worth it once the fish are found. Midwinter perching is always more enjoyable, thus, if you have a good sharp ice drill or, better yet, a power auger.

PERCH LURES

On big, shallow lakes where cruising schools of perch are common, I still like jigging up perch on Russian Hooks or similar, large-size jigging spoons. Art Best once offered me tips on using these lures, and I paid close attention.

"I think colors make quite a difference," Best told me as we watched anglers work perch on Lake Huron's Saginaw Bay, a regionally-known hotspot for perch action, summer and winter.

"In my opinion," Best said, "the most consistent fish-catcher is a red-and-white (Russian) hook. Other good color combinations are fluorescent yellow with a red dot or pearl with a red dot. Sometimes plain copper works best in dark water."

Those color tips have paid off for me many times since, while other anglers swear by pearl in dark or muddy water, silver or bright copper in waters that are clear. Some even carry steel wool to brighten up a lure that's lost its luster.

But red remains a color common to many popular winter perch baits. Some of my best deep-, clear-water perching has come on a far-smaller red tear-drop shaped lure, baited with wax worms or small minnows. Red teardrops easily outfished offerings in other colors.

PRODUCTIVE TECHNIQUES

Best added to his perch catches by tying a short piece of red yarn so that it extended about a quarter-inch on each side of the hook, with the ends frayed. He wasn't sure just what the yarn resembled to a perch, but it's a safe bet it somehow acted lifelike to the fish, known for eating just about any-thing.

How you fish for perch will depend in large part upon where you fish for them — in deep lakes or shallow waters.

In waters of eight feet and more, concentrate your search in the bottom couple of feet. You can use spoons, but for deepwater fishing most prefer a small ice fly or tear-drop-shaped lure baited with a small minnow or grub bait, such as a waxworm or mousie. Wigglers are also good baits.

For panfish-style teardrops, follow the panfishing

approach: jiggle the lure slightly, including a slight lift, then let it rest. Watch the bobber or spring-steel strike indicator and set the hook when you sense a strike. You may have to delay the set a little if using minnows, to allow the perch to take the bait deeply, but I've lost more fish (and bait) by waiting too long than by setting the hook too soon.

You may not need a lure at all; many perch fans use plain hooks or "perch spreaders," rigs that offer two snelled hooks above a bell sinker that rests on bottom.

If using minnows on a plain hook, good catches can often be taken without doing much jigging at all, especially if the minnow remains lively. It's still a good idea to lift the line periodically and allow it to settle back into place. I don't know if a lurking perch thinks his meal is escaping, or if the fluttering minnow draws in perch from afar, but a lot of hits come shortly after a movement of this type.

Whatever rig, but especially with minnow-baited lures, keep a tight line and work toward a light touch; perch are among the sneakiest of bait-stealing fish. They're neither fierce strikers nor flashy battlers; often you'll feel just a slight tug at the bite and little fight on the way up.

The perch's penchant for bait theft has made popular the use of real or artificial perch eyes for bait. Real perch eyes are the most effective, I believe.

Make sure to humanely kill the fish first. It takes awhile to learn to insert the hook of a lure into the eye and smoothly twist it out, but it's a skill well worth learning. Not only are the eyes effective as bait, they're virtually indestructible. You can fish for an hour or more without having to remove gloves and change baits. Best maintained that the more tattered the eye-bait, the better it worked. He'd fish an eye until there was little left of it.

Lure action? You'd best vary that until you find the cadence that produces fish on that specific day. Sometimes perch will nail only lures and baits that are lifted a foot or higher, then allowed to flutter back down. Most takes are on the downswing, so keep your attention riveted to the line.

On other days the panfish like best a slight wiggle of the

Figure 9 — A mitt-protected hand hoists a chunky perch caught on a Russian hook.

lure every few seconds. Sometimes no action is necessary; some of my biggest perch have come not on jigging rods, but on stationary tip-ups baited with minnows for walleyes or pike!

Locations? There again, you're going to have to experiment. The shallowest I've ever found perch was in 18 inches of water. The deepest came from 90 feet down.

Some of the best perch fishing in the world is found in fertile waters less than five feet deep, especially on big, shallow waters of larger lakes. In those regions icewater perchin' means tying on a Russian Hook or other large spoon and jigging in those shallow waters.

Using a Russian Hook is simple. Many anglers begin fishing with a hook baited with a minnow, switching baits to perch eyes once a few fish have been iced. Others use artificial, rubber perch eyes and report almost equal success. The key, simply, is to keep the lure moving and let the spoon's action draw in perch. Hooks of all sizes work well, although when fish are finicky it helps to jig a large spoon and offer a smaller spoon, other lure or minnow-baited plain hook to the fish in the same hole or one nearby.

Over shallow waters you might want to pinch down the barb of your hooks. That allows you to pull the perch atop the ice, shake it off the hook simply by bouncing the fish's tail on the ice, and relower the bait to the productive water in quick, smooth sequence. If using this barbless hook approach, try pressing a short piece of rubber band (try red!) onto the hook after the bait. That will dramatically reduce the theft of your bait by the hungry, sneaky perch.

Spoon-jigging for perch requires a special approach. Typically, this is a shallow-water tactic, and most veterans use rather stout rods wound with heavy line, often 15-pound test or even heavier. Perch just aren't line-shy like other species such as trout, bluegills and crappies. And just as perch like to follow schools of minnows, northern pike and sometimes walleyes often follow schools of perch, ready for a quick perch dinner. Stouter line offers you better odds of saving your lure and icing a toothy pike or lunker walleye if one can't resist the bouncing, shiny lure. And the heavy gear won't cost you any perch.

But perch remain your prime goal. Just keep the lure moving and set the hook when you feel a little extra weight or the tap-tap-tap of a feeding perch. Yank the fish atop the ice and get back into business after another. But don't go overboard with the jigging if no action results. Keep the lure moving, but try slowing the pace if the action is slow. Sometimes that works wonders. If not, try a different hole.

Since perch are schooling fish, you want to catch as many as possible before the school moves on to other spots. Happily, the more you catch the longer the action seems to last. Many perch fans say that as long as food — your bait included — appears available, the perch will remain. Once there's no food nearby, though, they'll continue searching for it elsewhere. That puts a premium on keeping your line in the water as much as possible.

Some serious perch anglers even fish two lines in the same hole, just so that there's always something to hold the perch's hungry interest. That's only practical in shallow water, however.

Another approach is to use a double-lure rigging. One perch-fishing friend of mine likes a double-hook rig including a large, shiny spoon a foot or so above a smaller, baited lure. "Most of my fish are caught on the smaller hook," he says, "but the big lure seems to draw them in." He also baits up first with minnows to get the action underway, then switches to perch eyes or other baits that can't be stolen as easily by the panfish thieves.

We mentioned perch or crappie rigs in our deepwater discussion; they're productive in the shallows, too. These offer two plain hooks on separate leaders. A bell sinker at the bottom of the rig anchors it to the bottom. Bait each hook with a minnow, wiggler or grub, and lower the weight. Snug up the line, watch that line, and feel for a tap. Set the hook before the perch has a chance to steal your bait and escape.

Many perch pros like any method that keeps their success as secret as possible. Often you can work a school of nice-sized perch for a half-hour or more, provided that ice-top noise and vibration is kept to a minimum. But if less successful anglers nearby notice that you're collecting a nice mess, they're apt to come a-calling, complete with snowmobiles, power augers and enough other noise to move the fish to another area. The veteran perchers are often able to catch a dozen or more perch without even their closest fishing neighbors noticing, using a minimum of arm movement to fight their fish, quickly depositing each fish in their bucket with a minimum of fanfare and generally keeping the good fortune a secret.

If you're the lucky fisherman, learn to be sneaky. If not, try using a pair of binoculars to locate action nearby. Don't stomp right into a successful angler's fishing grounds, but try moving into the line of travel the perch appear to be following. You might be able to intersect some memorable angling.

You might be lucky enough to find a school of chunky perch under the first hole you drill, but it's far more likely that you'll have to cut a dozen or more holes and walk across a lot of ice to locate those first keepers, especially over shallow water. And even then, you'll likely want to try a different spot when that school has moved away. I know a few anglers who, having found perch under a couple of holes, will loyally wait for them to return. Usually, eventually, they will. But few of us have that level of faith and patience. Most of us feel the urge to find our fish instead of waiting for them to find us again.

We've already mentioned that perch are schooling fish, moving as a group from one feeding location to another. Remember, too, that these schools also generally contain fish of the same size. You may not want to spend much time catching and returning tiny perch — but you'll sure want to cash in when the 8-inch and larger "slabs" are biting!

Once ice reaches thicknesses of six inches or more a good, sharp hand auger or power auger is indispensible. And if using the power auger, find a sled or tobaggon on which to pull it. A long day's perch fishing seems to add to the weight of a gas-powered auger when it comes time to head back to the car.

Home again, get ready for a treat. I once treated my college roommate to a mess of freshly-caught perch from a deep, coldwater lake. They were good enough that he, an inveterate golfer and thus more attuned to hot weather, gathered warm togs and tagged along on the next ice-fishing trip. He wasn't disappointed, either. Once again the perch, averaging about seven inches each, cooperated. Another fish fry was the happy result.

I fillet my perch, slide my knife between the meat and skin, roll the skinless fillet in pancake flour and simply fry it in hot grease or oil.

Other anglers, those lucky enough to catch a truly big mess of perch, do a quick fillet job with an electric knife, lopping off the fillet complete with skin and rib bones. They place the meaty chunks in water, freezing them into a block of ice as-is, to trim out the bones and, with a knife, peel off the skin when the fillet thaws. That appreciably shortens the fish-cleaning time after a full day on the ice.

Still other fishermen prefer simply to remove the fish's head, entrails and fins, and fry up their perch.

However you like your perch, you're probably among the millions who rate them the best-tasting species of all. And I'll bet you'll never find them tastier than when caught from this winter's batch of icewater.

Many times I've savored the dual pleasures of winter perch fishing — the sport of catching and enjoyment of dining. For either, you can't beat icewater perch. They're almost always hungry, numerous and, for most anglers across ice country, nearby. Among the most prolific, cooperative and tasty of fish, they're the winter angler's true friend.

Figure 10 — A lake trout lays atop eight inches of clear, black ice, and alongside the tip-up on which it was caught.

Chapter 6

Settings

Part 1: BLACK ICE, MAGIC ICE

Crunch! Your reaction is involuntary. You leap halfway off the five-gallon plastic bucket upon which you're seated, quickly looking around to see if anyone's noticed. Sheepishly, you hunker back down, eyes returning to the thin line and tiny bobber.

You know, after all, that the ice is safe. You examined it carefully at the shore, kept checking it all the way out, then worked up a sweat spudding a hole through it. Those are all rational facts lodged in the brain, though. Jumping when the ice pops is an instinctive physical, not mental, reaction.

It's early in the ice-fishing season, and the ice is just freshly formed. It will take a few more outings, at least, to make it again seem natural to roam the tops of lakes on foot.

Boom! The lake's at it again, moaning as its own surface waters seal it off even tighter. Cracks form a complicated, spider-web design and your heart, not your brain, makes you suspicious of each hairline slit, even though it's in ice four, six or even twelve inches thick.

A nearby tip-up releases its flag. You hustle towards it, almost skating on the soles of your felt-pac boots, now tossing only a stray thought to the ice upon which you move.

The reel's spinning as you bend down, and you nervously remove the tip-up from the hole in the ice. A buddy's next to you, ready to help in any way he can. Clumsily you grab for a temporarily slack piece of line and lean back on it when it tightens. The battle's on.

Dozens of times this winter you may wage a war with a fish, but seldom under these unique conditions. For long before the fish is near the hole, you not only know it's a trout, you know it's about a four-pounder.

How? Well, your partner has wandered about 50 feet away from the hole, and he spied the trout through the clear, 10-inch ice cover. Laughing, he's chasing the fish, and every detail of that fish and its flight is clear to him.

When the fish finally flops atop the ice, it's against the dark backdrop of 60 feet of water behind a window-like plate of ice.

This is a special kind of first ice — black ice. It's the best ice. I'm inexplicably drawn by its magic. Black ice — freshly-formed stuff so clear it makes your heart pound, but still strong enough to keep your feet dry. Fishing through it can be the most productive of the winter season, for reasons we'll discuss a little later. But fish are only half the equation. The angler is the other half. And, without scientific backing, I'll wager that ice fishermen — most ice fishermen, anyway — work harder at their sport than do open-water anglers.

After all, the ice fisherman's not combining his sport with suntanning or some other fair-weather pleasure. I love ice fishing, but I'll concede a winter lake-top can be a physically uncomfortable place to be. There's darn little reason to sit in the cold, snow and wind unless you're serious about your fishing. So serious, in fact, that you'll watch your line closer and move around more willingly in search of fish.

Fine fishing, then, is a big part of the draw of early-season ice fishing — but only part. Sure you can be confident that fish are beneath you on first ice but you're not only sampling the best of the lake's fishing, you're enjoying the best of the lake. Just as the freshest snowfall is always prettiest, the first blue-sky spring day always the most appreciated, the freshly-frozen lake is always the most impressive.

It's on that lake that you're struck with the very special privilege you enjoy in the lone ability to walk on the waters. Later, you'll be distracted by ice skaters, candy wrappers, fishing shanties and snowmobiles. Even cars.

Now you're alone. You're almost a pioneer. This season's hotspots won't be discovered unless you help find them. There's no hard-packed trail leading to a shanty-town. At most, you may spot a dozen or two fellow-anglers, likely spread randomly across the lake. And, if you're like me, you'll always be just a little bit frightened about being alone on a big, winter lake.

Frightened, by my definition, is anywhere between carefree and scared. If you're at either end of that word-game spectrum, I'd suggest staying off first ice.

If you're scared, perhaps there's good reason. If you're completely worry-free, maybe you haven't checked the ice closely enough. You need at least three inches of good, hard ice to walk safely and fish alone. Four inches is a lot better, and the minimum for on-foot anglers fishing near each other. The rules are simple, and so's the fishing on that first ice.

Part of ice fishing's fun comes from that simplicity. By the time ice arrives I've parked the fishing boat in the garage, its motor, recording graph, downriggers and similar fancy gear in hibernation for a few months. I've traded all that for a plastic bucket of tackle and a spud. It really matters little what that gear includes — tip-ups for trout, pike or walleyes, or jigging rods for bluegills, crappies and perch.

Just choose a basic rig, test the ice, and taste the sweetness of the early season. Fish are more likely to forgive your technical errors now than at any point in the season.

The fish seem under a spell now, too, just like the fishermen who seek them. I'm not sure what draws the fish to the other end of my line when lakes first freeze over. But I know why I'm there: it's the black magic of black ice.

Figure 11 — The season's first ice can provide a platform for memorable catches, such as this nice mess of crappies.

Part 2: FIRST ICE

Black ice and first ice aren't necessarily the same. Clear, black ice — a window to the world below and a slippery platform for the angler above — occurs on only a few lakes and, even on them, only every few seasons.

First ice, logically, comes to every frozen lake every year. And while not the rare stuff black ice is, first ice is to be appreciated, too. It may be black or grey, smooth or covered with snow or maybe even slush. Still, it's special.

For the calendar really isn't kind to the ice fisherman. Grouse season opens on a certain date, pheasant season on another. You can find the opening day of the deer or stream-trout season on a calendar. But ice-fishing season doesn't open until Mother Nature says so.

So fans of the ice begin watching puddles in November, hoping that ever-colder mornings leave them with a skim of ice. Only then can we rationally begin digging out tip-ups, jigging poles and augers. And we must still wait many weeks more until small lakes, then larger bodies of water, freeze-over solidly enough to support our fishing efforts.

We've stressed safety already. Don't go on a lake you're unsure of. But safety is the only question facing you now. For anyone who's sampled the pleasures of early-season ice fishing knows full well that the fish will be there and biting just as soon as we can get out.

I once asked a fish biologist why early-season first-ice fishing is so much more productive than any other fishing of the season. He explained that winter brings a cooling down of water and a shut-down in the lake's food factory.

Those changes really begin in fall, when less sunlight reaches the water each day and temperatures begin to drop. When winter deepens, panfish and larger predator fish will trim their activity levels to match the conditions in which they live. But smaller organisms and plants seem to feel the changes first, leaving panfish and gamefish still in the midst of pre-winter feeding while food supplies become scarcer.

So tip-ups fly often for fishermen working first ice for northern pike and walleyes. Crappies and bluegills often keep a panfisherman so busy that he can only keep up with the action of one rod, even though most states allow him to fish with more. The first few weeks of safe ice are the only time I've ever caught a largemouth bass through the ice (they're legal until Dec. 31 in my home state of Michigan, and there's almost always ice fishing available by then). We once even iced an early-ice carp of about seven pounds. It grabbed a tear-drop and wax-worm combination intended to catch bluegills.

Yes, the calendar's cruel to the ice fisherman. We've ice-fished, tentatively and admittedly seldom, just a few days after Thanksgiving when winter arrived early a couple of years. Usually, but not always, we've been on safe ice by Christmas Day. But whenever it arrives, the start of the ice fishing season is something you should not miss.

That's why I get ready early.

It used to be that the first ice outing would find me on the ice mumbling — auger or spud dull, tip-ups tangled up, jigging rods wrapped with rotten line tied to rusted lures. No longer does first ice find me unprepared, and probably for at least two reasons. One, I've discovered that an hour's work in the basement can save a day's troubles on the ice. I don't want to compromise the best fishing of the season. Second, I now get so excited about the coming ice fishing that, by October, I've generally dug out and fixed up the tackle.

You don't need much in the way of equipment for early-season fishing. Since ice hasn't yet thickened much, a spud is handier than an auger, and a good safety precaution as well. You must assume that early ice is never safe. Use the spud to whack the ice in front of you as you proceed onto the lake. Cutting a test hole to check the ice's thickness is a good idea, too; just don't do it where other anglers are likely to be walking.

You probably won't have to venture far onto a lake now to sample its action. Crappies and bluegills are often in water less than 10 feet deep, and those depths are often good for pike and walleyes as well.

The simplest early-season fishing is for panfish. This time of the year crappies and bluegills seem to form large, mixed schools, and the first-ice action they provide can be frantic.

The fishing is easily worth the effort required to watch those driveway puddles as they begin to harden in fall, worth the gas to double-check on your favorite lake even before you think ice could have formed.

For there's no opening day for ice fishing. Someone will always get on the lake before you. Let them. Make sure the ice is safe before you risk your life for a bucket of fish. But make sure, too, that when the conditions are safe, you're there and fishing. The calendar may be unkind to the ice fisherman, but Mother Nature is generous with her fish when the ice season finally opens.

Part 3: SOCIETY ON ICE

A few times each season I walk onto a lake on which I can see no other human beings. That can be an unsettling feeling, something like walking into an empty department store or parking in an empty lot.

Where is everybody? Is the fishing absolutely dead or, worse, does everyone but you know that the lake is unsafe? Has the Department of Natural Resources closed the lake to fishing or has the season ended?

Usually the desertion is just a matter of coincidence. Nobody's fishing today, and there's nothing more sinister involved.

And for every day you spend on an empty lake, there'll be countless others on which you'll find more than ample company on your favorite body of water.

Coping with the society on the ice can sometimes be as challenging as the fishing.

What can you say, after all, when you're fighting a fish

Figure 12 — Fishing shanties — and anglers in the open air — gather where the fishing's good. Provided you mind your manners, there's almost always room for one more.

on a tip-up, your partner walking the tip-up away from the hole to keep the monofilament in a straight, untangled line, and a snowmobile approaches?

There's no sense yelling at the driver, for he can't hear through the heavy hood and helmet. And there isn't time to tell him that, if he continues on his present course, he's going to cross the six-pound test you've been mothering so carefully. In seconds he snaps the light line you've been treating so gently all season.

You smile weakly, wave, and forget the vengeful notion of spooling heavier line and holding it chest-high the next time a sledder comes by.

The tightest form of ice-fishing society is found in a shanty. In these outhouse-sized structures parties of up to four fishermen mix their fortunes next to a heater. The wind howls outside but the fishermen are oblivious. Sometimes too oblivious.

One friend still tells the story of a shanty that stood against a harsh north wind on a large lake. The walls shuddered against the wind but held firm. The base of the shanty, however, hadn't yet formed a tight bond to the ice. As it broke free the three anglers inside poured out of the door, their heaviest coats still inside the coop. And they helplessly

Figure 13 — This chocolate Labrador retriever was caught in the act of stealing a bluegill.

watched as their home-away-from home ice-boated across the lake.

We all know that social graces are a key to functioning in a civilized society. Ice fishing is a touch less civilized, and perhaps the society is a little less gracious.

If you ask a gas station attendant for directions, you assume he's telling you the truth. But ask an ice fishermen how he's doing, how he did yesterday, or even what he's using for bait, and it's even money he's fibbing.

"They killed them out here yesterday," one oldtimer told me on a small bluegill lake one winter day. "Four guys were out here all morning and they all limited out." He didn't know, obviously, that I was one of the four, and that we got skunked.

Kids and dogs are part of the society of ice fishermen. I know a spot where you dare not leave a fish on the ice, for a German shepherd is almost always lurking nearby, eager to eat a crappie. A friend's Labrador retriever loves three things in life — retrieving downed ducks, stealing fish from ice fishermen, and wrapping itself in light monofilament line. He's praised for the first, cursed for the last and forgiven by its red-faced owner for the middle.

Kids are even less predictable. And they're infuriating. They often pay the least attention to the fishing and catch the most fish. They can dress in blue jeans and tennis shoes and stay warm. You can give them the most slipshod tackle and they excell with it. Their first question leads to an interrogation, and they can smell a tall tale a mile off.

A great twist on the challenge of ice fishing is to see how big a whopper of a story you can get a kid to swallow. But do that only if the kid belongs to someone else. If the kid's yours, answer the question in depth. Maybe some day he'll remember your patience kindly and take you fishing.

Part 4: TWO-FLOP DAYS

There are all types of ice fishing days. There are great days and bad days. There are fun days and work days. There are balmy days and, yes, there are two-flop days.

Through most of the winter the ice fisherman really doesn't suffer very much. Folks at home may shudder with the thought of their loved ones at the mercy of the elements on a big, wind-swept lake. But the truth is that, with modern cold-weather clothing and a decent pair of felt-pac boots, 95 percent of all winter days provide pretty comfortable fishing.

They feel comfortable, anyway, compared to two-flop days.

My first two-flop day was spent on a lake from which we'd been extracting crappies with stunning regularity. Palm-sized and larger crappies would seemingly line up for turns at the tear-drop lure baited with a wax worm, and early each day a pile of those tasty panfish would be flopping against each other on the ice.

But this day was different. We first noticed it when we walked onto the frozen lake and, instead of feeling our hands and feet warm with the exertion of a quarter-mile hike through the snow, we stopped to pull hats lower over our ears and zip up coats.

The breeze — or more acurately, wind — struck our faces with the force of an angry woman's slap. Undaunted, we settled over the "hot" fishing holes we'd first punched a few days earlier.

The spud made short work of the two inches of ice that had formed since sundown the preceeding day. And pulling the four-pound test monofilament between gloves seemed to take the cold-induced kinks out of it. The wax worms were stiff, but rolling them between the fingers — in the few seconds we allowed those digits to be exposed — restored the bait to softness so they could be threaded onto a hook. Now we fished.

I didn't really pay too much attention to the first few crappies we iced. They were coming atop the ice at the same rate we'd enjoyed in previous days. But after a half-dozen had come up, I noticed there was no movement on the pile. A nine-incher struck my lure, was elevated to ice-top, and joined the pile. It flopped once at full-strength, again half-heartedly. Then it appeared to freeze solid.

"Who needs a thermometer?" my friend asked. "We know it's a two-flop day."

Temperature readings do mean little to the ice angler. I've been cozy at 10 degrees when the sun shone and the winds lay still. And I've darned near froze when winds pushed 35-degree air over the lake. Messers. Celsius and Fahrenheit never bargained on that.

So we fixed upon the flop scale. Anything higher than three-flop is a blue-ribbon ice fishing day. After the third flop, in fact, I quit counting. On such a day ice won't form at the top of the minnow bucket. Checking tip-up holes every 15 or 20 minutes will ensure they'll stay open enough that you can easily extract the tip-up if a fish hits. Ice will be slow to form on your jigging-rod bobber, too, so that you won't often have to suck on the float to remove enough ice to allow you to fish efficiently.

The three-flop day just lets you know how good you've got it. A gentle tap will puncture the skim ice sealing your minnows in the bucket. After an hour's fishing you might slip on your gloves for a little warming before returning to bare-handed fishing. You might even leave the hood of your parka down, needing it only along the back of your neck to protect this seemingly chill-prone section of your anatomy.

That hood comes up on a two-flop day, but you won't likely pull the drawstrings tight. You'll wear gloves more than half the time, and you'll make sure your back is against the wind. If there's a shanty nearby, you'll probably decide that the best fishing spot is just downwind from that shelter.

Woe to the angler who heads out on a one-flop day. When the bluegill, walleye or trout freezes after just one wiggle on the ice, you can stand to remove your gloves only briefly. On this day the wind seems positively mean-spirited — blowing in your face on the walk onto the ice and coming around 180 degrees to dish out the same punishment on the way back in.

Thin monofilament line seems to roll into knots easier on this kind of day, and you'll wish you brought extra fishing rigs so that you could untangle fouled ones at home. On a one-flop day your feet quit stinging after an hour's fishing — and it's only an hour after you quit that you find they just went numb. You know you're getting warmer on a one-flop day when your feet start hurting again.

There are also no-flop days. We were heading 80 miles to a trout lake one morning when we heard on the radio that a neighboring school district's classes had been canceled because of the arctic conditions. A regular fishing buddy taught in that district, so we decided to stop at his house and invite him along, even though it was only 6 a.m.. Aware that we'd planned to fish, he was watching for us out the living room window when we pulled into his driveway.

It was cold on the lake. Simply, painfully cold. Minnows froze in the bucket, and tip-ups were locked in ice in 15 minutes. But actually, after the first big chill the anglers fared relatively well. We fought fish with gloved hands — when the tip-up reels spun freely enough that the trout didn't simply break the four-pound test line. And — believe me — when the trout we caught hit the ice they never flopped, quivered or anything. They quick-froze, pure and simple.

We tended tip-ups for several hours before surrendering to the harsh elements. One bearded fisherman had felt his breath freeze on his mustache and beard until the two were fused together by ice.

Another gave up after having spudded two tip-ups free of the rapidly-forming ice just to check them.

And those two found your author in the small car, trying to thaw two frozen cameras on the defroster.

We turned on the car radio and discovered that, at high noon, the actual temperature was 20 below zero and the chill factor 50 below. Pulling out of our parking space we heard a strange noise from the back seat. "One of the trout just flopped," said Tom. "It isn't a no-flop day after all."

Part 5: LAKER COUNTRY

The lake trout seems to have little to offer this high-powered angling age.

We've planted Pacific Ocean coho and chinook salmon in the Great Lakes and other inland lakes such as South Dakota's Lake Oahe. Rainbow trout from the Pacific now swim in dozens of states, Atlantic salmon in Midwest waters and beyond. Brown trout came here from Germany.

Immigration aside, we've swapped bass, walleyes and trout from lake to lake. We've even built some of our own fish — striper/white bass crosses, pike/muskie hybrids and laker/brookie crosses and backcrosses.

Figure 14 — The author proudly hoists three nice lake trout, taken a long walk from shore.

Many of those glamour species offer plenty. The hybrid striper provides unbridled fight. The splake is easily caught and a tasty delight. The tiger musky grows quickly to provide top-flight fishing action.

The lake trout, meanwhile, just hugs the bottom of its native lakes. Known regionally as the laker, togue, mackinaw or grey trout, it feeds pragmatically upon whatever living or dead matter it finds. It may take four growing seasons or more for that prowling to produce an 18-inch fish.

The laker is not particularly fierce in battle nor stunning on the table, although it performs credibly in both areas.

Much of the laker's magic comes from the places where you find him.

The mackinaw thrives only where lakes are deep, clear and cold. Those regions are home also to whitefish, ciscoe and others, but the laker reigns, the top consumer in the food chain. It's a dark, coldwater world 100 feet or more below the surface, down where water temperatures are in the low 50s. Togue thrive there; you'd be hypothermic in minutes.

Laker angling is as unusual as the quarry itself. As an angler you generally don't get close to a lake trout until you've fooled him. Most fishing is from at least 70 feet above the trout, often double that amount or more. That's a long line of faith running from your fishing rig to the lure or bait. And since typical laker lures dance and weave wildly below the ice, grey trout fishermen can't sit shoulder-to-shoulder as can perch or panfish fans; lure-holding lines would become quickly tangled.

So laker fishing is a relatively solitary pursuit — a heavily-clad fisherman perhaps a few dozen yards from his angling partner and likely a few hundred yards from angling neighbors outside his party.

That's the barren social setting, and few of us would have it any other way. For all the fanciness we build into our equipment and strategies, we still like simple fishing. You either offer the laker a live or dead bait suspended on a tip-up or other stationary fishing device, or you bob a lure, baited or unbaited, and hope to attract the fish's interest.

Either approach is limited to the last few feet before bottom, and it's an even-money bet that hours may pass before the action takes place.

Laker anglers are a little different than many of their fishing brethren. They're not quite as action-oriented as panfishermen or pike fans. They are — and must be — a little more willing to watch smoke curl smoothly from the chimney of a cabin on shore, tracing the path of that smoke as it snakes through the pines and onto the lake.

Most gray-trout fans who bob lures can't even tell you what action they gave the lure just before a strike came; they were hypnotized by the cadence and the setting, and the strike surprised them, maybe more than the hook surprised the trout.

Laker fishermen are almost required to enjoy watching an entire shoreline disappear in a snowstorm. On certain winter days, from a mile out onto a big, deepwater lake, you can watch a haze move over a lake. Slowly the quality of light changes. Dark colors get darker, more intense, while light shades grow lighter, clearer.

About the time the scene has nearly faded to black and white the snow arrives.

The first few flakes zip by quickly. You check your coat sleeve for proof it was snow, maybe ask your partner if he's seen it too. The cloud slowly moving offshore at lake-level appears half-haze, half-precipitation, and you quickly double-check the compass heading back to the car. For you've been here before.

You know that in a few minutes the red cabin to the south, that small one behind the tall pine, will start to fade from sight. There — the stored snow just blew out of the big tree, adding fuel to the mini-blizzard moving towards you and your tip-ups. The other cabins along the lake are now beginning to fade away, too. They don't just disappear; they literally wash out. The snow in the mile between gradually builds in intensity and the picture becomes less distinct, finally disappearing.

You may be a little uncomfortable at first when only a

compass links you to your car, its heater and, eventually, home, but there's not much you can do about it now. And once the shore's gone, a certain home-in-the-wild feeling arrives.

Suddenly it's not so cold, and you're somehow more confident in your ability to handle what nature throws your way. You grab the skimmer and ladel slush from the fishing holes. You gather the scattered gear so it won't become snow-buried and lost. And you settle back down to watch, alternately, your tip-ups and the ghost of the shoreline.

Even in the heaviest of snows, the shoreline will fade back into view from time to time. And eventually, the snows will slacken and the cabins pop back into view.

More times than not, that'll happen before you've finished fishing, and you'll be almost sorry that it has.

If you don't like watching the cabins fade away, I'm betting that you won't much like lake trout fishing. For the laker is prized as much for what it is and where it lives than for what it does. The laker's a rather solitary fish in a rather harsh environment. So, too, is the lake trout fisherman, albeit only for a precious few hours each winter.

We can ship, produce or even create better fighting, better eating fish. But the laker's a native of these big, deep, wild waters, and he somehow makes you feel at home atop them.

Figure 15 — A young angler proudly hoists a northern pike.

Chapter 7

Northern Pike

What has more teeth than a cross-cut saw? More enthusiasm than a 10-year-old on his first fishing trip? More fight than your little brother or sister? It's the northern pike, the big-game species most often identified with ice fishing.

The northern, after all, is no piker. My battered desk-top dictionary defines a "piker" as one "who does things in a small or cheap way." That description just plain misses the northern pike completely. He's a warmwater eating machine — deceptively slow when he likes, lightning-fast when he prefers. He's equipped with a mouth filled with teeth that can make short work of whatever he attacks. And that's a long list of things — from minnows and worms to mice, ducklings and even legal-sized gamefish.

If what a pike strikes strikes back — like the hook hidden within a minnow — the pike's fight is impressive. There's just nothing a pike does, harking back to the dictionary, that's done in a small or cheap way.

Whether you watch a tip-up, waiting for its red-flag indication of action, jig a shiny lure in hopes of a strike that can slam your knuckles into the ice, or tend a spear inside a dark shanty, you'll end up voting for the northern pike as the prime minister of ice fishing.

The pike is a member of the Esox family of fishes. So, too, are the muskellunge, several species of kindred eating machines. There's even a cross between a northern pike and native musky called the 'norlunge' or tiger musky. Check your state's rules on taking these critters; often there's a larger minimum size limit on muskellunge, and in some areas they can't be kept at all in winter time. But if the muskies are fair game, follow the same tactics we outline for pike, just upping, perhaps, the size of the baits and strength of tackle and to match their bigger size and meaner — if that's possible — disposition.

Any description of a pike must include the tooth-filled mouth, sleek and powerful body and insatiable appetite. The first two serve the latter. You'll guard against the teeth and power but cater to the appetite.

Pike, like the panfish we discussed earlier, provide for a variety of fishing methods and approaches. You can rather casually set a minnow-loaded tip-up for pike while jigging for crappies or bluegills nearby, or you can pursue the pike vigorously and on its own merits, tending tip-ups or other rigs solely for them. Either way, the northern pike is likely to cooperate. But you can tip the odds further in your favor, in any of several ways.

Pike will eat almost anything, from minnows to gamefish, from worms to ducklings. Stick with baits from the fish family, however — minnows, suckers and smelt — and you won't go wrong.

Let's talk tip-ups first. I'd guess that more ice-time pike are caught each year on tip-ups than on any other kind of tackle. (As a side bet I'd wager that tip-ups catch more pike than any other species, too. The method and fish seem made for each other.)

A tip-up is simply a device that holds your bait a certain distance off the bottom, keeping a springy flag compressed until the reel turns to release it to an upright position. What turns the reel is the fish you're after.

After that simple description there are dozens of style variations. Most tip-ups consist of crossed sticks that lay horizontally and hold the tip-up above the ice. The reel is submerged, and is set to engage a wire lever if turned by a fish. That wire runs vertically up the center stick of the tip-up, and releases a bright red flag on a springy piece of metal when the reel turns.

I'm fussy about the tip-ups I use for lake and brown trout through the ice, and picky about the ones I use for wary walleyes. But pike just aren't that delicate. They won't automatically drop the bait if they feel resistance. They'll yank it until it comes free. Just about any commercial tip-up made will catch pike. It's what you do with it that counts.

My ice-fishing tackle collection includes several tip-up designs. One is the standard, inexpensive tip-up with a metal reel about two inches in diameter. Frankly, I haven't use that style of tip-up in years. For a dollar more you can get a tip-up with a larger, plastic reel. The larger reel illustrates a law of physics that it takes less force to move a large wheel a short distance than to move a smaller one the same distance. On a tip-up the pike doesn't have to pull as hard on the bait to release the flag, and the lesser resistance makes spooking fish far less likely. But pike aren't very spooky anyway, so that's just part of the reason.

The real reason I like a bigger reel is that it's far easier to put line back onto the reel after the fight. The plastic reels almost always come with handles that make line-winding easier. Since they're larger it takes fewer cranks to get the job done. And plastic doesn't feel as cold to the (usually-bare) hands as does metal.

Of course I have other styles of tip-ups, too. One, originally purchased for deep-water fishing for trout, has a plastic reel about five inches across. You don't need a reel that big for pike fishing, of course, but you'll never find it a handicap. Tip-ups with large reels are versatile; with a few tackle changes, they'll do a good job on any fish that swims in ice country.

I've even found one style of metal-reel tip-up I like. But that's a 20-year-old design made in Michigan. Sad to say, I don't know where or if they are available now. I found my three at a yard sale, and they're among the small portion of my ice tackle that I won't loan out to anyone.

First, these metal reels are about three inches in diameter. That's just right. And the real beauty is in the way the tip-up mechanism is designed. Instead of a stick, the upright is a metal tube. Inside the tube is a spring-loaded shaft. It tucks under a tab on the reel at the bottom and holds the flag at the top. But instead of simply cradling the flag by an L-shaped hook, as do most tip-ups, this peg is inside the upright tube, visible through a small hole in the side of the tube.

A hole in the flag shaft fits over the post, so the hook-up is contained within the tube.

The result is a tip-up protected from the wind. "Wind flags", those releases that come only because the wind has blown the flag free, just don't happen with these. When a flag flies, you can be sure it's because a fish swims underneath.

I've tried other tip-ups and rejected them, often on rather whimsical grounds. Like a wooden creation in my ice fishing bucket that holds the flag on a stick of wood that in turn balances upon a wire lever. If mine is typical, the wind blows the flag off five times for every one time a fish is responsible.

I've tried wind-powered tip-ups, too, those that use the wind to impart a soft jigging action to the bait. But every day I took one along it snowed so hard that the mechanism wouldn't work correctly. When I didn't take it the weather was lovely. It only took a dozen or so trips to decide to leave the wind-powered tip-up home and enjoy fine fishing weather.

There are also aluminum tip-ups that hold the underwater reel parallel to the ice instead of perpendicular to it. They work well, especially those with adjustable set-off weights. They're good for walleye fishing and will work well for pike,

Figure 16 — Stout tackle, including heavy line like that pictured here, can help tame a pike caught from stumpy impoundments.

too, although gear this fancy isn't absolutely essential. They won't, however, hold enough line for deepwater trout angling, if you're trying to assemble basic equipment for fishing all season for all species.

All those tip-ups designs discussed (and there are many others), here's the plain truth: Just about any commercial tip-up available will work to take pike through the ice. Your choice depends mainly upon how much you want to spend, how long you want the tip-up to last, and how many species of fish you want to catch with it.

Just as with tip-ups, there's an infinite variety of terminal tackle available to the pike fisherman. Every serious pike fisherman I know is specific about the type of rigging he uses; nothing else is acceptable. But there's a lot of variation between these "tried-and-true" set-ups.

Begin with a length of stout line. Some anglers like black braided line, others gear up with more expensive (and higher quality) low-stretch Dacron. Others still wrap on heavy monofilament, and I've even seen tip-ups loaded with sinking fly line. Just make sure you have about 50 yards of good line on the tip-up. And while it's not absolutely necessary, 25-pound test gives plenty of room to apply leverage in a fight.

In my part of the country a 10-pound pike is rare, and rarer still is the northern I can't land on 8- or 10-pound test nylon monofilament line. Since that's how I gear up for other species, that's what I use for pike. But pike aren't line-shy as are trout and walleyes; wrap on heavier line if you like.

The biggest variation between tip-up pike rigs comes in the last couple of feet of line. To ice these battlers you have to protect your line against the teeth, and there are a couple of ways to do that.

Traditionally, most pike fishermen use a steel leader six to l8 inches long. Some braided wire leaders come coated with nylon, some don't, and I don't really see where it makes much difference. The leader most often runs to a fairly large treble hook, and generally the line carries two or three split shot just above the point where the leader's tied to the main line.

Thousands — make that millions — of northern pike have probably been caught on this rigging through the years. And more will continue to be caught. But I can't help thinking there's a better way.

Part of the reason I feel that way stems from the first several winter pike I caught. Near my home is a river impoundment known for its early-season panfishing. We can almost always get on the lake before Christmas, once as early as late November. And the bass season here runs through the end of the year. So there's always the temptation to set a tip-up with lighter tackle and a small minnow for bass or wall-eye, while jigging for panfish with the other line we're allowed by law.

The double-focus works, but that's not really the point of talking about it here. It just seemed that every time I rigged up light for bass and walleyes — with six-pound test line, a small treble hook and a small minnow — a hungry pike would come along and grab the bait. Maybe six times in ten

I'd coax that pike onto the ice. Two of the other times the fish would somehow escape the hook, and the last two times the line would break against the sharp teeth of the pike.

Now, at this same time of the year, some other anglers turn to this same lake for some serious pike fishing — setting their steel-leader-equipped tip-ups and landing a higher percentage of the fish they'd hook. They'd land almost every pike on their line, but I'd have many more flags than them, and ice at least as many in a full day's fishing.

Even while jigging for panfish, offering tear-drop lures baited with wax worms on four-pound test line, I'll sometimes feel the heavy pull of a nice pike, and more than once have slid a nice one onto the ice, caught on light gear and a rod with no reel.

It's commonly accepted that pike aren't line-shy as are some other species. But I think there are times when you'll have better luck by scaling down your tackle. Maybe the pike are spooked a little by a heavy leader; maybe, too, the difference is in the way your bait acts. Unencumbered by a heavy leader, the minnow can swim more freely, naturally.

Sometimes, then, you can boost your pike action by foregoing steel leaders.

There are times, sure, when you just plain need stout gear to stand a chance of landing a pike. I remember well a day spent on the upstream stretches of a large river impoundment. Water was shallow and stumps plentiful. And quite frankly, if you didn't have line of 25 pounds test and a businesslike leader, the pike would take out enough line to wrap you around a stump, leaving you with a broken line and battered spirit.

(The friend who guided me to this spot even lost a nice pike when it snapped a heavy steel leader in two. When you tangle with these big, mean fish, some are going to win the fight. That's a big part of the lure of pike fishing, after all.)

So there's a place, then, for both ends of the spectrum of pike fishing tackle. If you're going to fish one body of water most of the time, set your tackle up for it — lighter gear if there's plenty of room for fights and pike that run a little small on the average, stouter stuff if the lake's cluttered and the pike large.

For most of my pike I now favor a leader of monofilament of about l0- or l5-pounds test, a couple of feet long. It's less visible than a steel leader, but still strong enough to stand some abuse from the fish, provided you take enough care during the fight. And it doesn't matter too much what the backing line is, as long as it's heavy enough to allow you to put some force on the fish.

There is a good argument for braided line, since it is easy to handle during a fight and less apt to tangle on the ice. Still, my tip-ups stay wrapped with mono. I've just never had enough problems with it to switch.

Minnow-type baits are best for tip-up fishing. If live bait is available and legal, use it. It has the taste, smell and look that pike like, at the activity of a struggling bait often bring pike a-running, so to speak. Rig up with a treble hook, and that hook needn't be especially large. I've caught many pike on tiny size 12 trebles, and have never had a hook bend open far enough to grant a northern its freedom. Even if you give up a little strength with a smaller hook, rest assured you've made a good bargain on hooking ability.

It's easy to demonstrate the difference in ease of hooking. Imagine yourself in a doctor's office, waiting for an innoculation. You've a choice between a big needle and a small one. Which would you choose? Or let's say you're building something from wood and can choose between using a handful of small nails or an equal number of large ones. You know that, as long as they're big enough to hold, the small ones will be driven home easier. It's the same with fish hooks; the smaller the point and shaft, the easier it penetrates the hard mouth of a fish.

Golden, blue and gray shiners are good, especially in sizes of four inches and up. Big sucker minnows are the favorite of many trophy pike specialists. And pike often seem to delight in polishing off a live smelt. Pick a hook size to match the size of the bait, but, again, don't be afraid of small, light-wire hooks.

I like hooking live bait just under the dorsal fin. The bait stays alive and active for long periods, hangs in a natural level position even when inactive, and by the time the bait's half-way down the pike's throat, the hook is firmly in its mouth.

Fishing with live bait isn't always possible, however (or even legal, in some states). Don't despair — just bait up with a dead offering. Remember, pike are eating machines; they'll eat just about anything. You can hang a dead minnow in the manner described above, and chances are good a pike will accept your offering. But a friend showed me a method that works better yet.

That friend uses triangular-shanked hooks known variously as Swedish or Norweigan hooks. They hold a dead bait perfectly level and, when the line's pulled sharply by the angler, the point of the hook pivots, driven home into the roof of the fish's mouth. Rigging is simple. Insert the point through the anal opening of the bait and run it out through the mouth.

If mixing live (treble-hook) and dead (Norweigan-hook) rigs, keep track of which is which. They require different fishing methods. Many pike fans rush to the tip-up when the flag flies, hoping the reel's still turning. They wait for a pause, then strike when a second run begins.

With the dead-bait, Norweigan hook rig, however, such a wait is neither needed nor desired. No pike is ever going to swallow that big three-sided hook. And you want the fish moving well when you set the hook, since the big point requires more hook-setting force.

My friend walks gently to a tip-up when a flag flies. He waits for the fish to move away from the hole and — wham! — he sets the hook soundly. He wants a quick fight on the shortest line possible, a concession to the stumpy waters in which he fishes. Make sure you don't allow the pike any slack line, since the hook is as much levered into place as it is hooked.

Here's Dave Read's logic behind the slow approach to a tip-up: "A pike doesn't run after taking a minnow in its natural setting. He just moves away a little bit and enjoys his meal. He only runs if he hears or feels you coming. If you're fishing where there are a lot of stumps (which we were) you don't want him to get any further out than necessary." So Read walks quietly to his tip-up and, as long as the pike is moving, slams the hook home.

Of all the big, dead baits offered to pike, the sucker is probably the most popular. But the smelt may just be the most effective. Veterans swear that the oily smelt gives off some of that oil when resting in the water. And since fish locate their food by smell and taste as well as sight, pike zero in on this tasty offering. You can catch smelt through the ice on large, cold, deep lakes, keep some frozen in the freezer from the spring runs many areas enjoy, or even buy them dressed in a grocery store. Pike don't care.

Whatever bait you run on your Swedish or Norweigan hook, make sure you set that hook hard. You're driving a large hook through a large bait fish, then into the tough mouth of a pike. It takes a big tug to get the job done.

The big-hook system works well. It's a real killer on pike when fishing with dead bait. But it does require some special tactics, so keep them in mind all the time you're on the ice.

Where do you fish for pike? That's a complicated one. I've caught them from three feet of water and have friends who've iced them from 90 feet down while fishing for trout. They're a mobile fish, found wherever there's food available. Generally, though, shallower water pays off best. Start fishing near drop-offs and weed beds, where pike have both food and cover available. Pike favor a blend of shallow-water bait-fish and cover in the form of vegetation, brush or deep water.

I'd start setting tip-ups (as many as the law allows) in waters from 6 to 25 feet deep. And I might not set them all just the way you'd think.

Several expert pike fishermen of my acquaintance have casually mentioned that they feel many winter pike fisher-men are missing the boat. "Did you ever look at a pike's head?" one of them once asked me. "Their eyes look up, not down. So where do most ice fishermen put their pike bait?

Yup, right on bottom, or within a foot or two of it. If a pike comes cruising along the bottom, they just might see your bait and take a swipe at it. But if the fish comes in higher than that, looking above him for his next meal, he just might miss your offering completely."

Another friend, one who spends many hours each winter watching from a spearing shanty for pike, said many of the fish he pokes are just under the surface of the ice. So that's where he hangs his tip-up baits.

Try this the next time you're northern pike fishing in waters 20 feet deep or less: run half your party's tip-ups near bottom, in the customary range most pike anglers work. But set the others about as deep as you are tall. I'm betting those will get the lion's share of the action.

Generally, I'm no big fan of gaff hooks for ice fishing. They do come in handy for pike, however. I land fish of most species just by reaching into the hole and cradling the fish's body with my hand and flipping it atop the ice. Sometimes, on a larger fish, I'll grab for a gill cover. But those moves are more difficult and dangerous when you're dealing with a toothy pike. Better to start the fish's head up the hole when it's pooped, then gaff it cleanly and lift it the rest of the way out of the water.

Make sure, though, that it's of legal length — that you're not mutilating a fish the law requires you to release.

DANCE A JIG

I'm an ice fisherman of wavering allegiances. There's darned little that competes with the excitement of seeing a tip-up flag fly at long last, as far as I am concerned. But one of the few feelings that's as enjoyable is the hammering strike of a big fish slamming a lure. Want to try a different twist on pike fishing? Dance a jig.

My first pike on a jig came in open water, and I was fishing for perch. I was attending a meeting near a large, inland lake. Since I hadn't planned on fishing, I was short on tackle.

I found a casting rod and some shiny silver spoons in the trunk of my car, and with them headed out to the first drop-off to try for perch. Instead, I rowed back in an hour later with a three-foot-long pike in the bottom of the boat.

I'd guess that most jig-fishing pike fans started in a similar manner — catching a big pike while fishing for something else. But they stay hooked on jig-caught pike.

Spear-fishermen say a pike moves in to consider a spearing decoy, lurking just offstage and choosing its own moment to move in for the kill. That it does with abandon, and that's the instinct you're counting on as you jig for a northern.

Jigging has several advantages. It's mobile, for one; you can quickly work a half-dozen holes or more. It's also active. And, most dramatically, you're on a direct hook-up to a close-in pike.

Gear up with an outfit that lets you pay out line. Use a reel-equipped ice-fishing jig outfit, or a short casting rod and reel. Forget steel leaders; they hamper the action of your lure. Many lures take pike through the ice; the best-known include Swedish Pimples and jigging-model Rapalas. But don't hesitate to try the spoons so successful on pike in the open-water months, the red-and-white Dardevle tops among them.

Line should test about 15 pounds. Any less and you risk breaking off the fish at the hook-set; any stronger and it will cut the action of the lure.

Pike seem especially apt to strike a lure when it's lying at rest between jigging motions. So let the lure rest occasionally. But much of the time keep varying the cadence, force and depth at which you jig the lure. Cover all depths patiently before moving on to another hole.

Jig-caught pike do strike hard. We sat on an impoundment watching tip-ups one sunny winter day, and the discussion turned to jigging. Two of us had caught some nice lake trout a few days earlier by bouncing spoons off the bottom. Finally one of my partners pulled a tip-up (to stay within the legal limit on the number of lines), grabbed a jigging rod, and began bouncing a Dardevle off the bottom four feet beneath him. He and the 24-inch pike were equally surprised when the strike came a few minutes later. The fight was brief on the short line but the effect was lasting; all three of us became instant fans of jigging for pike.

Another long-time pike fan gears up with a sinking fly line on a jigging rod. This line is strong, of a neutral color, and sinks quickly. It doesn't freeze up as easily, either. To it he adds a three-foot leader of heavy monofilament. He concedes that tip-up fishing may be slightly more productive, but jigging is infinitely more exciting.

When jigging for pike, try to stay ready for a strike all the time. But I've a strong hunch — the result of pleasant experience — that you'll get a smashing strike when you least expect it.

The northern pike — teeth, muscles and appetite —is a mean customer. You can test his prowling hunger with a tip-up or challenge him to a brawl on a jigging rod. Either way, he's ready for action. You'd better be!

Figure 17 — Walleyes, considered by many the tastiest of fish, bring smiles to the lucky ice fishermen who catch them.

Chapter 8

Walleyes

Walleyes are seemingly the ultimate quarry of the ice fisherman. They're distributed about as widely as pike. They school like perch and resemble their striped cousins in their preference for a diet of fish. But they're also as wary as brown trout. And no fish can top them for taste on the table. When ice-fishing prizes are compared, the walleye is almost always accorded first place.

It takes more planning, effort, inconvenience and luck to catch walleyes than just about any other icewater species, but their elusive nature and gourmet flavor combine to make all that worthwhile.

One morning we parked a pickup truck at the end of a snow-filled logging road. One car was already parked there, and its frosted windshield indicated it had been parked there for a few hours.

We gathered our pike-fishing gear from the back of the truck, silently congratulating ourselves on getting up so early and getting a really early start on our day's fishing.

The first rays of sunlight were just starting to trace multi-colored fingers in the sky when the bright beam of a gas lantern bobbed over the top of the high river bank down which we planned to walk to a pike hotspot.

Two fishermen appeared, one of them carrying the lantern and the other lugging a plastic pail that was obviously laden with fish and tip-ups. The tails of three fish stuck out from the bucket; they looked like 18-inchers, anyway. "How'd you do?" our surprised fishing host asked the fishermen. "Got a few walleyes," came the response, once the first fisherman was sure we'd already seen their fish. He unlocked the back of the frost-covered station wagon. His partner quickly stashed the bucket in the car, without letting us check out the catch.

"That's walleye fishermen for you," our pike-fishing host muttered. "They can be downright anti-social."

Walleye fishermen — good walleye fishermen — beat the sun to their favorite spots and often watch tip-ups against a sunset background. Night-fishing's fairly common, too, among the stout-hearted. Walleye fans don't often join in the daytime gatherings of pike, panfish or trout fishermen. And when they find a hotspot, like the backwater bayou on which we planned to catch pike, they generally keep it to themselves, preferring not to let others get a glimpse of their good fortune.

Does that challenge appeal to you — trying for a wary, wandering fish that requires delicacy balanced by persistence? Then the walleye's definitely your fish.

I first learned walleye patience on a big inland lake. I'd joined a fish biologist for an evening of walleye fishing. He promised to teach me how to connect with walleyes. And if you ask me, he didn't have to wait so long to make his lesson.

Jerry warned me in mid-afternoon that it might be dark before the efforts paid off. Sure enough, the couple of daylight hours remaining when we reached our fishing spot a mile or so offshore brought us fishing action — but only on small northern pike and a perch or two. Meanwhile we fine-tuned our tactics and fueled our enthusiasm.

Two basic approaches catch most mid-winter walleyes. Jigging a light line baited with a lure or live bait is always a good way to connect with walleyes. Watching a lightly-set tip-up baited with a small minnow on light line is another.

When Jerry finally showed us some walleye catching, it was on a rig that combined the best of both worlds. A friend of his had developed a machine he called a tip-down. A short spinning rod is held in a cradle, with a little clip to hold the line at the base of the stand. The bail of the open-face spinning reel is left open, the line is held in the clip, and the rod set with its tip pointing more up than down.

The bait is a two-inch minnow impaled on a small treble hook, with just enough weight added to hold the minnow down.

It takes little pressure for the fish to pull the rod to a position below horizontal, then peel line freely from the reel. The angler is then free to fight the fish on rod and reel, just as would the jigging fisherman.

Just as the sun dropped behind the western shore of this big lake the unusual fishing set-up went into action. "Here we go," Jerry shouted as I fumbled to pull a camera out of the bag and attach a flash unit to it. It was really getting dark.

Jerry fought the walleye several minutes, then eased the 17-incher through the ice. "That's all there is to it."

Of course, there's more than that to catching walleyes in the winter. You have to understand these fish. You have to remember their tendency to feed in low-light periods — at dusk and daybreak and, often, in the nighttime in between. You have to track their movements through the season and through the day. You must scale down your gear for these wary fish. And, most of all, you must have the patience required to wait for them.

Walleye will sometimes give you a big head and a bum steer when your favorite warmwater lake first freezes over. Then 'eyes, like most other fish, are more active than they'll

Figure 18 — Walleyes usually bite best during low-light conditions, with action sometimes good even at night.

be for the rest of the winter — eating whatever they find, at just about any hour of the day. You can get spoiled, and sloppy. About the time you do, midwinter sets in. And that season is not a forgiving one.

Of all the variables that affect ice fishing for walleyes, time of day is one of the more crucial. All-night fishing doesn't really get too many takers — either fish or fishermen. The best periods for walleye fishing are just before dark or just after daylight early in the winter. In midwinter I'd rate the two hours after dark and the two before daylight as best.

Northern Lower Michigan's Houghton Lake, the state's largest inland body of water, is regionally well-known for walleyes. A local group even rears young walleyes to planting size in a nearby pond, releasing them in the lake when they've reached sizes at which survival is likely. Combined with the lake's natural reproduction, the fishing that results is first-rate.

Ron Reed owns a resort on Houghton Lake and rents shanties to ice fishermen from all over Michigan and beyond. Between his fishing and that of his customers, he knows what works on walleyes. He fishes the first and last hours of darkness, and uses two fishing systems with success.

Reed said his most productive approach to walleyes is with a jigging rig. He uses a sinking fly line for the main line, "because it doesn't freeze up as easily. And I add a three-foot leader of eight-pound test monofilament." The line is wrapped on a single-action fly reel. Best lures include Swedish Pimples and Jigging Rapalas, both in size five. "Fish one to two feet off the bottom," Reed advises, "and work up to three feet off bottom with quick jerks to let the lure work." He said his best jigging success comes the first hour of daylight each day and from an hour before dark until two or three hours after dark.

You can connect on walleyes by running a straight jigging line of four-pound test monofilament line, too, or by offering small spoons like those used for perch. Remember, after all, that walleyes are members of the perch — not pike — family.

To cash in on the walleye's preference for fish, add a dead minnow, the tail or head of a minnow, or even a flap of skin cut from a fish, to the lure. Like perch, walleyes haunt deeper waters in daylight, shallower when light drops. Walleyes also tend to travel in schools, though not often in the tight packs in which perch are found. Don't be surprised to mix perch or pike into your catch, either; some of the best walleye catches I've seen were part of mixed bags.

Reed said some of his best walleye catches on tip-ups come in full darkness. He rigs with light line and small hooks and sets tip-ups close enough to him that he can set the hook before the fish can drop the bait.

Tip-up fishing anglers often connect when it's still light, too, but usually only if they've scaled their line down to around four pounds test and chosen tip-ups that release easily and smoothly, without telegraphing the fish of the trouble ahead.

My walleye tip-ups are invariably lined with four-pound test wrapped onto carefully-selected tip-ups. Less-expensive rigs with small metal reels may be okay for pike fishing, but I don't use them for skittish walleyes. A larger reel requires less pressure to release the flag, and its smoother action makes it less likely the fish will spook as it takes the bait.

To improve my odds further I tie on light-wire treble hooks in size 10 or 12, and clamp on only enough shot to keep the bait underwater. One small split-shot is often all that's required for the 1^1/$_2$- to 2-inch minnows I prefer.

A rigging variation is to run the line from the tip-up through a small, egg-type sinker, then tie it to a barrel swivel. Add a leader two or three feet long running to the small treble hook. When a fish hits, the sinker falls to the bottom and the line feeds smoothly through it. As a result the fish can take out line without feeling much resistance.

Walleyes hug bottom, so you'll want a clip-on weight for finding bottom and adjusting your line. Then add a tiny clip-on bobber to the line just at water level. When your flag releases the bobber helps you tell if there's a fish 'on', since a false release will leave the float within view. Whether the flag produces a fish or not, the bobber makes it easy to re-set the rig at the same depth.

Want an argument? Ask two walleye fishermen when to set the hook. Chances are one will warn you never to yank the hook home until the fish has made one run, paused to swallow the hook, and begun another run.

Others will swear the small hook will find its way home as soon as the flag goes off. I've seen plenty of fish landed (and lost) using both systems. It's up to you.

There's less disagreement on the best places to find winter walleyes. Mainly fish-eaters, their food supplies are the weedbeds and shallows of warmwater lakes, but they like spending non-feeding times in deeper, clearer waters. You'll want to intercept them between the two areas.

Many veterans know from summer and winter experience where main weed beds are located within a lake. (That's how my friend selected the spot at which we caught the fish described at the start of this chapter; I learned later that he triangulated the position by mentally tracing lines from the spot to landmarks on shore — but he didn't disclose the markers to us. Walleye fishermen, remember, are protective of their best fishing grounds.) If you're new to a lake try to find a map showing weedbeds, or coax the info out of an oldtimer on the lake or in a baitshop. It's a long shot, but it could be the key to your first walleye fishing success.

Walleyes are also big fans of bottom structure — any change in the contour of the bottom. Rocky points are probably the best-known of "classic" walleye hotspots. But the structure can be far more subtle. On one large bay I know, you'll find walleyes wherever the bottom changes — even where a reef rises just a foot above the surrounding bottom. Pay special attention to underwater points and reefs, along with other sharp dropoffs.

If you can figure out both ends of the walleye's movement pattern — the deeper water in which it spends most of its day and the food supplies to which it turns at evening and daybreak, try working several locations between the two. Don't use more than the number of lines your state allows but spread your angling party along the daily migration route. If one person seems to be getting more than his share of the action, join him.

But do so quietly. Walleyes aren't bold. It takes a quiet, lightweight approach to fool these fish. And they're worth the effort — both flopping on the ice in the rays of a fading sun or lantern, and popping in grease on a hot stove.

How long should you wait for walleyes? That's a tough one. During one recent season two anglers stopped by my house to show off a midwinter catch of walleyes.

With a third partner the pair had made a trip to a well-known walleye hotspot, a large bay on one of the Great Lakes. Bad weather kept them off the ice for a week but when they finally got out one morning, they limited out with 15 walleyes, most of them in the four-and five-pound class. One weighed $8^3/4$ pounds. All were caught on Swedish Pimples or blue and white spoons. Was the week too long to wait? Not for winter walleyes like that, it wasn't!

The walleye is almost universally popular among anglers, both summer and winter. In many places the limiting factor on walleye fishing has been the inability of local waterways to produce fish in numbers sufficient to support a fishery. Happily, that situation seems headed for a change.

WALLEYES FOR THE FUTURE

I recently watched two guys catch twelve pounds of wall-eyes in one morning. That's a good catch, right? Well, this catch was half what they'd caught the day before. Still, it included more than 5,000 walleyes —each of them less than two inches long.

The pair "caught" the walleyes in min-Fyke nets from a sewage treatment pond. The pond was doing double-duty by serving as a home for young walleyes for several months. It produced 80,000 walleye fingerlings for the nearby lake, plus several thousand for neighboring lakes. It typifies the dramatic increases ahead in walleye opportunities.

Walleyes were once among the most difficult of fish to raise. But biologists found a system that works well — and we can expect to reap benefits of that discovery for decades to come.

Drainable ponds are the key. In spring the empty pond is planted in a cover crop, then filled with water. Technicians add a treatment of yeast to promote a heavy bloom of plankton, the main food of young walleyes. The tiny fish — obtained from fish hatcheries and described as resembling little more than a needle with two eyes — are added and watched carefully. They grow to fingerling length in the ponds, a length at which they have good chances of surviving after release. That release must be timed carefully, since walleyes become canibalistic. At plant-out time the pond is lowered, the fish caught and transferred to their new homes — usually a lake nearby.

Once released the small walleyes require about three years to reach lengths of 15 inches. Where there's plenty of food and little competition, that length can sometimes be reached in just two years.

The sewage treatment pond where I watched technicians reap a walleye harvest required a slightly different approach. Draining the pond to collect the walleyes was impractical, but the Fyke nets efficiently captured the young fish. In hours they were swimming in a new lake, beginning the rapid growth that would in a few years endear them to fortunate ice fishermen.

Walleye rearing ponds are pumping more fishing excitement into inland waters every year, with more on the planning boards. Within a couple of years lakes and rivers near them can be expected to provide hot walleye fishing action. One fishery biologist involved in walleye rearing told me, "We'll never be able to meet the demand" of sport fishermen for more walleyes. "We're trying to select lakes that have potential, size, and geographic distribution." But the more walleyes planted, the more anglers want. And once you slide your first walleye through the ice (and take it home and fry the delicious fillets) you'll be wanting more, too!

Figure 19 — "Making do" can provide basic fishing equipment, or it can simply showcase the creativity of the ice angler.

Chapter 9

Making Do

Art Best once described for me early perch fishing on Saginaw Bay. Best, who most concede first successfully marketed the modern "Russian Hook" perch fishing spoon, wasn't on hand when ice fishing began on that large body of Lake Huron in east-central Lower Michigan. But he was able to trace part of the development of its fishery.

That fishing no doubt began long before white settlers arrived, with Indians catching fish of all kinds on the most primitive of gear.

But when Best arrived on the scene in the early part of this century, he found that the most dedicated and skilled of anglers were Russian immigrants who had come to the area to work in the growing and processing of sugar beets. They turned naturally to the nearby Bay for some combination of recreation and food-gathering, probably leaning rather heavily toward the latter.

It wasn't easy for anyone outside this tight circle to learn about the Russians' successful fishing methods, Best said. They'd wear long coats, hanging to their knees or beyond.

When they huddled over their fishing holes the big coats made tent-like screens that hid their efforts. And when asked any questions the immigrants — whether because of jealousy or a language barrier — made no reply. The silent Russians just caught perch, much to the frustration of less-successful anglers nearby.

Finally, though, the highly-successful immigrant anglers' secret got out. They needed raw materials for making more of the spoons they guarded, and the only sources to which they could turn were the sugar factories sprinkled across Michigan's "Thumb" region. Workers in those factories quickly figured out why the Russian guys needed metal — they were hammering out large metal spoons with which they were extracting buckets of Saginaw Bay perch!

Soon anglers all around the Bay were pounding out the spoons. Many, following the Russian lead, simply fashioned long, tear-drop-shaped lures, with the narrow end of the tear-drop rounded inward, and the very tip bent slightly outward again to form a rudimentary hook and barb. Others simply soldered onto the spoon shape a regular single-pointed fish hook.

Best first saw a Russian Hook in 1936, on a duck-hunting trip from his Wisconsin home to Saginaw Bay. "A fellow gave me a hook and showed me how to use it," he told me in 1978 at the age of 77. "I caught quite a few perch with it, and soon began to make a few of them." In the meantime he moved to Detroit for a factory job, and soon began marketing his spoons in his spare time.

The part-time business paused for World War II, which made metal for such frivolous items scarce. After the war Best moved to Sebewaing, along Saginaw Bay, and set up full production of his fishing lures. Before he sold his business in 1963 he had opened another plant in Ontario. And in less than three decades, by his best estimates, he sold a million Russian Hooks. They're still sold by the thousands every winter by the Best Tackle Company.

Other, similar success stories could be told of and by dozens of tackle inventors and fishing gear companies.

They're all interesting tales from the worlds of fishing and business.

But to me the most interesting aspects of these tales are the points they make about the ability of the ice fisherman to "make do" — to analyze a problem, figure out a solution, and then improve on that solution.

Let other, more organized minds trace the business developments. I'll be happy imagining how those Russians first discovered that perch would hit oversized, hook-shaped slabs of thin metal. I'll smile, picturing them guarding their secrets on the wind-swept ice. And I think I know the exciting feeling the local anglers must have felt when they finally discovered the spoon that has led to the demise of so many perch ever since. Then, up stepped Best, ready to convert his lure-making hobby into a business to supply the demand for the deadly lures.

The story is mirrored in all types of ice fishing equipment. For if there's one thing that successful ice anglers consistently exhibit, it's ingenuity. It's as if the very best ice fishing equipment is made at home, at little or no expense. If it's a copy, that's fine. If it's a truly original idea — which most describe as very rare indeed — that's far better yet.

That's why an ice fisherman will walk right past a bucket of two-dollar ice-jigging rods in a sporting goods store, only to hurry home and build one of his own, based on a slight improvement he's dreamt up. Maybe the improvement has actually improved the concept, maybe not. That doesn't matter. It's the effort, the imagination that counts.

You won't save much money following that angler's example, but you'll have a lot of fun. Some of your experiments may not work out, but maybe a few will. It's a lot like tying your own trout flies for warm-weather fishing — catching even a small fish imparts a real feeling of accomplishment.

And maybe — just maybe — you really do have an idea for which the ice fishing world has been waiting. Bring it on!

For now, though, you just want to build a jigging rod. That's easy enough. Remember that spinning rod that somehow jumped in the way of a closing car trunk last summer? It was severed right above the mid-rod ferrule, right? And even though it looked like just so much junk, you saved it just in case it might come in handy for some project or another. That project is now at hand.

(And if you can't find that rod tip, check the house plants. More than one angler's wife has learned that rod tips make wonderful plant supports.)

You can simply drill out a piece of dowel rod or broom handle, the hole just about the size of the large end of the rod tip, then glue the glass (or, if you were so unfortunate, graphite or boron) tip in the hole. Buy some cheap L-shaped hooks at a hardware store, screw them into the handle a few inches apart and with the L's facing away from each other, and wrap your fishing line between them. You're ready for panfishing!

For a fancier touch find a friend with a wood lathe and, before assembling the handle and tip, turn the handle into a piece of art. Cork handles are a little more sensitive, but assembly is correspondingly more difficult. I've had good luck wrapping the rod tip with masking tape until it's about the same diameter as the hollow, pre-formed cork handle, then glueing the two together. The result, just that quickly, is a short spinning rod. You can then attach a simple, line-holding bracket, or clamp on a reel. (We'll talk more about spin-fishing through the ice later.)

If you have to start from scratch, not having had the good (?) fortune to have broken a fine spinning rod recently, you might want to try building a rod from the whippy post that holds bicycle safety flags. Don't swipe the one from your kid's bike, though; the safety flags really are a life-saving measure for bikers. Make or buy a handle, glue on a tip-top and wrap on a guide or two if you wish, and you have a super-light action ice rod that will turn even a small bluegill's fight into a real adventure.

(A late fishing friend of mine even took that principle a step further. He built a seven-foot spinning rod from a bike flagstaff, clamped on a light spinning reel, and took on open-water steelhead trout. He held two different world records for steelhead caught on two-pound test line!)

I've never tried making my own tip-ups, but I've met plenty of others who have.

I once met an angler on a frozen lake who was a machinist by trade. He had fashioned tip-ups from machined aluminum. He didn't bother with a flag, figuring he'd sit close enough to them to see the above-water reel turning when a fish took the bait. The reel was held by a mouse-trap-like mechanism that released very easily — just what he wanted for the walleye fishing at which he excelled.

In the preceeding chapter we described a "tip-down," used to offer crafty walleyes a deceptive treat, then to fight them to the ice. That's a nifty homemade project, too.

A container for gear is usually next on the ice fisherman's list. Most of these — and, likely, the best — are gathered or built by the fisherman to suit his special needs.

The milk crate has been adopted by many anglers. These square, plastic boxes are built to hold four one-gallon jugs of milk, but they'll hold a lot of ice fishing tackle, too. They're light, fairly-easily obtained, and have handles to make carrying easier. Don't try lugging one a mile, though, without attaching some kind of shoulder strap.

I guess the only reason I don't use a milk crate is the open, screen-like sides. I always seem to pick nasty fishing days, and I always lug along a camera or two. When the snow blows, milk crates and their contents are open to the abuse.

Fortunately, other gear-lugging options abound. One friend of mine, limited by past heart surgery to the way he can carry loads, uses an army surplus metal-framed back-back. The pack holds plenty, rides well, and leaves his arms free. The only time that arrangement is a bad deal is on first, last and otherwise borderline-safe ice; it's hard enough to recover from a fall through the ice if you can toss your gear to one side, harder still if it's strapped to your back.

Wooden boxes are standard for many ice anglers, and they work pretty well. A 10- by 12-inch box, maybe two feet high, will hold more gear than you probably need to take along, plus it will serve as a seat once you're fishing. Drill holes on opposing sides at the top of the box and attach a rope for a carrying handle or shoulder strap.

Wooden boxes are a little heavy for long treks onto the ice, though; better still to build small runners so you can pull, rather than carry, them onto the ice. The tips of cast-off skis make boxes slide well.

Which brings us to sleds and tobaggons. Regular sleds on runners are okay as long as the snow isn't too deep. Better, though, are inexpensive, plastic tobagons. They're dish-shaped, and just adding a bucket or box completes the rig. We even use one to haul a power auger onto mid-season ice.

My own favorite container is the five-gallon pickle pail. Actually, mine formerly held oil for a sawmill. But regardless of its previous life, you can reincarnate a plastic bucket into the handiest ice-fishing gear-lugger of all. They're the perfect size for up to half a dozen rods or tip-ups, some terminal tackle, a slush skimmer and even a camera or two. Lunch and a vaccuum bottle fit in, too. Keep the top, after trimming off the tabs that lock it in place. It makes a handy seat. You can carry off your fish in the bucket, then once home wash it so clean your spouse won't even mind its storage in the house.

The homemade ethic of ice fishing probably surfaces in no more striking an area than the construction of shanties and shelters. We discussed them a little earlier, but let's look at some of the room for variety.

I confess, first, that not long ago I had never looked closely at shanty construction. I'm an open-air fisherman, so I usually just briefly envy shanty dwellers their comfort while maintaining that my mobility brings me more success.

But recently I ran into a delightful pair of ice fishermen on an inland lake near my home. They had driven a compact pickup truck onto two-foot-thick ice and easily lifted a shanty from the bed of that truck, onto the ice. Already I was impressed with two features of their shanty: it was more than

Figure 20 — This shanty was constructed from castoff storm doors.

roomy enough for the two anglers, plus light enough for them to move easily.

The more I learned about these anglers and their shanty, the more captivated I was by it and by them.

I learned that Mike Govitz of Beaverton, Mich., likes to build shanties. Almost as much as — and maybe even more than — he likes to fish in them. And that's a lot.

The lightweight shanty Govitz and his partner unloaded from the truck had recently passed ownership — from Govitz to his partner. Mike was already working on a new design in his spare time. But, as the creator, he took me on a guided tour of this one.

"I made it out of old screen and storm doors," Govitz said proudly. "Want to guess how many doors are in it?"

I conjured up my best guess but was more than a half-dozen doors short.

He answered his own question with a laugh. "Not even

close," he responded to my wild guess. "It took 14 storm doors to make this. And do you know what the base is made of?" This time I had no idea, but Govitz had another laugh ready. "It's the top off a chest freezer."

Govitz had "made-do," and had a fine time doing it. And he'd made a mighty fine, practical shanty. He started with a basic floor plan — the size of the freezer lid — then dissected doors, using pieces of frame and panel to flesh in the sides. He used no specific pattern — just tacked on material where it was needed. He used sheet metal screws to secure everything, then applied silicone caulk to each seam to make the whole arrangement wind-proof.

To frost his ice-shanty cake he took the tin box to a van-conversion shop and had the interior spray-foam insulated. In all but the coldest weather only a gas lantern was needed to heat it.

Even heavy ice shanties are often upset when really stiff winds buffet them, so a lightweight aluminimum one must be almost bolted right down to the ice. Govitz had attached handles to each of the four corners of his lightweight shanty, about a foot above the ice. When the shanty is in place he drills a hole in the ice at each corner. Short pieces of rope are then tied to each handle, and each to a foot-long piece of 2x4. The blocks of wood are slipped under the ice and, when the ropes are snugged the blocks serve as sturdy anchors for the shanty.

The real beauty of this aluminum shanty is that it's so portable. Sadly, 'coops' left on the ice for the season seem prone to break-ins and vandalism. (For that reason don't leave anything valuable in yours.) Govitz (and now, his partner, the owner of the shanty) doesn't worry. The shanty goes home at the end of the day.

While we talked, the shanty builder described his current model, one built of light plastic over a conduit frame. It, he said, was built with one panel that was hinged to fold flat. That way he can place the coop on a truck bed or trailer, open that panel, and drive into the shanty a snowmobile or three-wheel vehicle. Once at the lake the vehicle can be used to pull the shanty onto the ice.

Those are just two of an infinite number of shanty designs, both of these made from materials others had thrown away. Other shanties (I've since learned to examine them closely and guess to their background) are made from everything from top-grade plywood to thrown-out crating, from insulation material to canvas. And they all work, albeit to varying degrees and for varying durations. Keep your eyes open and your imagination active. Chances are you can build the perfect shanty for your favorite fishing spot just by "making-do".

Most shanties have a source of heat, and that can be a source of danger. Carbon monoxide kills by poisoning; lack of oxygen can also take your life. Make sure there's plenty of ventilation any time there's a heater in the shanty.

If you're a portable angler, combine a sled and shanty. Build a wooden box about three feet long and a foot square. A conduit frame a few feet higher will support canvas on three sides, making a wrap-around windbreak that will do the job on all but the very coldest of days.

Other items of ice fishing tackle are also often home-made. Many are the spuds that have been made by welding an oversize chisel onto a steel pole. Some folks even fill part or all of the hollow handle with lead to lend more authority to each whack. If you have a welding torch, the raw materials and the interest, give it a try. For me, though, there are just too many good spuds available at sporting goods stores for less than a $20 bill.

You can often use some workshop effort to render a piece of ice fishing equipment more efficient, however. Thousands of cup-type augers lie idle in garages and basements across ice country, for example, simply because their owners either can't figure out how to sharpen them adequately or have abused or misused them to the point of apparent use-lessness.

A sharp spoon- or cup-type auger is a joy. A dull one is a

curse. Learn to sharpen yours, or pay a few bucks to have a professional do it right. Or try fixing it so it will never need sharpening again.

A friend of mine is a high school shop teacher and confirmed putterer. He solved his cup auger problems by buying a cant file and cutting teeth into the leading edge of the cup. First examine the cup to make sure it's still round. If not, toss it out. But if round, use a felt-tip pen to mark out the position of the teeth. A scratch awl works well, too. Make marks about an eighth of an inch apart, starting at the center. From each of the marks, imagine a line running from it to the center of the cup. It's like a bicycle wheel, with each tooth-line a spoke.

Now cut each tooth on the inside of the cup so that it points to the center. The file and teeth will follow the angle of the original beveled edge of the cup.

The teeth increase the cutting surface. So start with a small number of teeth, perhaps two or three inches' worth, and see how it works. If you put in too many teeth, it may take three of you to turn the auger. You can add more later, if need be.

I'm not sure I'd want to try cutting teeth in a brand new auger cup, but the method's worth a try before discarding an old cup.

Giving your spud a few licks with a file between trips can pay off with less work on the ice. Put the spud in a vise with the cutting edge on top. Use a draw file and grip it with one hand on each end. That puts one hand above the cutting edge and one below it as you draw the file across from side to side. You're following the original angle of the spud's cutting edge, my shop-teacher buddy told me, which in almost all cases is the best angle for the ice-cutting job.

If you want to use a gaff — which I don't, opting to let the fish that beats me at the surface gain its freedom — you can make a nifty one for ice fishing by welding a large treble hook onto a metal handle. Be sure to add a wooden or rubber hand-grip to the handle, to keep your hand from freezing to the metal. A wrist strap can keep you from losing the gaff, too.

You can "make do" with your own bait, too, especially for panfish. I like fishing for bluegills and crappies with grub-type baits. And I buy most of them from bait shops. But I've also used grubs cut from the galls of goldenrod stalks, on several occasions cutting them near lake-side when financially embarassed or too far from a bait shop. One friend gathers acorns and places them in a pail filled with sand. As the weather cools the grubs found within many acorns bore out of the nuts and burrow into the sand. A quick sifting and the bait's ready for fishing.

You can also cut corn-borers from corn stalks in which you see a hole. Panfish love them. A beekeeper may have a rack overridden by wax worms; if he doesn't ice fish he'll probably be more than happy to get rid of them — and you'll have a good supply of panfishing baits.

Whether it's bait or tackle, 'making do' is part of the fun. We've used a shotgun approach to show some examples; now it's time to turn your imagination loose!

MAKING DO, EMOTIONALLY TOO!

The ice fisherman's prowess at making do is well-known. Most now-common pieces of equipment were once the brain-children of enterprising, frustrated ice anglers toiling in workshops or garages, or even on the ice. Tactics borrowed from open-water angling have been adapted and, I think, improved.

But the ice fisherman's ingenuity has been overlooked when it comes to the nubbin, the very guts, of his penchant for the homemade — homemade diversion.

No sane outdoor writer, no matter how much solid how-to information he has imparted, would promise you fish on every outing. At least once in the next half-dozen seasons you're going to sit on a frozen lake while absolutely nothing happens. No bites. No tip-up flags. Nothing. Zip. Skunko. Your nose will run, your feet will freeze, and your brain will be only warm enough to entertain doubtful thoughts on the wisdom of your chosen sport.

"I don't have to sit out here and take this crap," a long-time fishing buddy has told me more than once. "Here we are, two grown men, sitting on a block of ice. The wind's blowing, it's snowing to beat the band, and the fish aren't doing anything."

Then, predictably, his face will brighten, a foolish grin stretching from ear to ear. I know what he's going to say — one more time — "Been fishing all day, 'expect a bite any minute."

Still, the situation is tense. We don't want to quit. A fish might just bite. Even if not, there are too many distasteful, worthwhile chores waiting at home if we arrive there early. It's time to fashion some diversion.

On one minus-20-degree day, two friends and I watched idle tip-ups on a river impoundment said to contain an abundance of big walleyes and northern pike. It likely still does; we sure didn't harvest any of them.

After several hours of fish-less fishing our angling egos had become badly bruised. Counseling would have told us we needed to assert our concept of self-worth. And, fortunately, the artistic muses awoke while the angling gods snoozed.

Dale started it all, walking away from the center of our tip-up spread through the fresh, deep, untracked snow. We watched in impressed silence as he walked a few steps in one direction, turned around for a few steps, then made a 90-degree shift and walked on. In a few minutes we caught on — Dale was signing his name in the snow with footprints. Fred quickly followed suit. Somehow I felt more foolish sitting on a plastic bucket on a frozen lake than I would joining in, so I slogged off in another direction.

I just nicely got my first name stomped into the snow,

however, when I realized both of my buddies had a patently unfair advantage.

Both of them had four-letter first names (mine has five) and, though not related, both were surnamed Smith (five letters, versus seven in mine). I evened the challenge somewhat by leaving an initial instead of a last name.

Despite my shameful shortcut, by the time that frozen morning's fishing was over I had taken show honors in our felt-pac-boot art contest by walking out a sketch of a girl I wished I'd known in high school. There was nothing obscene about the drawing; it was just another way to spend some extra ice-fishing time — busily if not productively.

And before I'd stomped arms onto the girl, one of the tip-up flags flew.

There's no shortage of other ice-top diversions. On a couple of occasions I've sampled snow-sleeping. On a certain kind of winter day the sun shines brightly although the temperatures stay cold. The winds stay generously calm. It's cold enough to keep the snow from melting but the sun's warm enough to remove fears of freezing to death. On those rare days — and it takes something of a veteran to spot one — you can sleep blissfully for an hour or two. Just make sure your partner's trustworthy — that he'll wake you up if your tip-up's active or if he's going home. I recommend keeping the car keys in your pocket.

Awake, I don't normally go in for the mean game of trying to set off my partner's tip-ups when he's not looking, simulating action with a shifty foot or snowball. But if he starts the contest I'm up to the challenge.

I'd rather take on that partner in a rousing game of ice (fishing) hockey. It's played a lot like regular ice hockey except that there is no puck, no sticks, no boards, no goals and no rules. You need only a frozen lake from which you've spudded a chunk of ice, ostensibly for access to the fish. The object is to kick the chunk of ice back and forth between you until one of the athletes decides it's been kicked too far to be worth going after. The other athlete wins.

An interesting variation is to keep kicking until the chunk of ice hits one of the tip-ups. This is top-level competition.

We've often thought of ice-fishing diversions too complex for everyday use; we're saving them for desperate times.

Why not try counting the minnows in your minnow bucket? This is a challenging task, especially if the baitfish are small and plentiful. If the fish haven't been biting all day, you probably still have enough minnows to put some sport in this. To get an accurate count you must devise some way to tell individual minnows apart to make sure you don't count the same one twice. Pick out a characteristic that separates each minnow from his friends. If you want, you can name each.

Here's a mean twist on minnow counting, and it requires a conspiracy between two members of an angling trio. Bet your in-the-know partner $10 that you can guess closer than he how many minnows are in the bucket. Once you've both guessed, assign the sorry third partner the task of actually counting them. Even if you lose it's almost worth $10 to watch him try.

Counting wax worms isn't much of a challenge. For real sport, stage a wax worm race. This isn't likely to become an Olympic or field-trial event, since the little fellows don't move terribly fast. One good race will keep you entertained through the biggest part of an angling day.

You can always play detective. Walk around to other fishing holes (abandoned when their smarter or more frustrated drillers went home to watch the ball game) and try to figure out which was the most productive. Cigar butts, tobacco spittle and dead bait are among the clues that indicate long-term angling success.

I've found holes with plenty of evidence and decided to try them myself, only to become convinced that it was drilled by a cigar chain-smoker who drooled and dropped minnows onto the ice just to be mean. I've had the feeling, too, that maybe he was watching from shore, choking back a laugh.

I've often thought that we need not even actually travel to

a lake for ice-fishing diversion. Remember the big boom in video games? Well, they never came out with ICE-MAN.

Here's the set-up for this video game: The walleyes are biting on a big lake but the ice is thin. Your player moves onto the lake, risking a fall-through. You have to choose a safe path and guess where the fish are lurking. Then you set up tip-ups and try your luck. The catch is that you only have two minutes to fish before heading home to put up storm windows two months late. In those two minutes you must catch your legal limit of five fish (no more, since the conservation officer zips across the screen occasionally). And if all that weren't challenging enough, you have to dodge speeding snowmobiles all the time you're on the ice.

I played that ICE MAN video game once. Or at least thought I did. Actually, I dreamed it while I was snow-sleeping. And when I awoke, thanks to a block of ice kicked into me by an angling partner 20 yards away, I saw my two tip-ups flags flying fraudulantly, our third partner counting minnows, and an obscene phrase containing my name stomped into the snow. "Been fishing all day," the ice-kicker laughed. "Expect a bite any minute."

A stout stick and heavy line is used to offer hefty chugging lures to lake trout.

Chapter 10

Trout

Many anglers equate trout with summer. They like best swatting mosquitoes and false-casting dry-flies. When cold weather comes they retreat to tying benches and fishing tackle catalogs and mark time until the following spring. They miss out on the very best trout fishing of the year — ice fishing for trout.

I get really excited about my trout fishing when the lakes — Great Lakes or inland trout lakes — freeze over. You can catch any species of trout through the ice with a minimum of gear and have a superb time doing it.

The first step is settling upon a quarry. On some lakes that's no problem, since the lake may offer only browns, only lake trout or only rainbows. But modern fish management has spread trout to more and more lakes, with some offering a variety of trout species.

One of my favorite lakes offers three species of trout, plus a salmon that's a close relative of the brown. And there you must adapt your tactics to fish you seek. No matter how many species of trout you have available, you have more choices in approaches to them.

This favorite lake holds good numbers of both brown and lake trout, two species that differ greatly in their habits and habitat. It also holds splake, a cross between lake trout and brook trout. That hybrid takes its name from SPECKLED (brook) and LAKE trout, and it behaves more like a laker than do any of the other trouts. To confuse the picture further, the lake also holds a small population of landlocked Atlantic salmon, closely related to the brown trout.

Lakers and brookies, after all, are actually members of the Salvelinus or char family, while brown and rainbow trout and Atlantic salmon belong to the scientific family Salmo.

But that's enough science for me. Let's catch them, then worry about their scientific identification later.

On any of the so-called trout species, ice fishing can be deadly. Through-ice angling, in fact, is so efficient, especially for lake trout and splake, that special rules are in force in many areas and on many lakes, restricting the methods and bait that can be used, the minimum size of the fish that can be kept, or the number that can be iced per day.

Lake trout are increasingly a concern to biologists who are beginning to ask such questions as: Are lake trout too easy? Can modern management keep up with fishing pressure?

Once you find lake trout, they're typically easy to catch. The result can be a heavy harvest of a population of lakers. On lakes where lake trout are planted mainly to provide fishing opportunities, that's okay.

But on lakes such as the Great Lakes, where state, provincial and federal biologists are hoping to re-establish self-sustaining populations of lakers, and on other big lakes where lakers were native, cutbacks in the yearly catch have become necessary.

In several states, closed seasons on Great Lakes lakers have been instituted, shutting off ice fishing for lake trout completely.

As this was written Great Lakes regulations varied. Michigan allowed no winter laker fishing on lakes Michigan and Huron; lakers were fair game on Lake Superior. Minnesota had instituted only a two-month fishing moratorium each fall. Wisconsin was looking to cut its daily laker limit from three fish to one or two. Indiana had cut its laker creel limit from three fish to two daily. New York anglers on Lake Erie were limited to one laker per day. They could keep up to three lake trout per day on Lake Ontario, however. On Ontario's provincial Great Lakes waters, there was no closed season on lakers from lakes Ontario, Erie, Huron or Superior, with a creel limit of three fish per day.

So are lakers too easy? That's still a tough call. Winter lake trout fishing opportunities on the Great Lakes — where many claim the sport was born — are likely to face continued cutbacks. Fisheries biologists, after all, maintain that even if lake trout were as challenging as coho and chinook salmon and brown and steelhead trout, that might still be too easy. For while those four exotic species are planted with the angler in mind — an investment made in the Great Lakes fish bank with a definite maturity date — the goal in planting lake trout is different.

Biologists want the laker reestablished as a native species in the natural niche it has held for perhaps thousands of years. To achieve that we may have to curb our sport catches further.

That still allows some winter fishing for Great Lakes lakers, however, and plenty more in those lakes in which lakers were planted mainly to provide recreational opportunities. You'll have to do some research to learn where winter lakers are legal near you, especially since some inland lakes managed just for trout have closed seasons. So double-check the rule book before heading onto the ice after trout.

And chances are you'll laugh at the above discussion when you begin fishing for lakers. When you've shivered on a big block of ice for a day, trying in vain to entice a lake trout to take a bait, you might not think they're too easy. But have faith; there'll be days when your limit comes atop the ice almost too fast. Learn a few different approaches to winter lake trout, and that day may come sooner than you think.

Two types of tactics take ice-time lake trout best. The first is the tip-up. Tip-ups consist of crossed sticks that suspend an underwater reel that holds your line and bait at a certain depth. When the fish takes the bait the reel turns, releasing a flag that summons you to action. There are many, many designs of tip-ups, from plain two-dollar models to some that flash lights, work on adjustable magnetic systems or bob the bait in a wind-powered jigging motion. Any will catch lakers.

Tip-ups catch probably millions of trout every winter across ice country. For all-round trout fishing I spool up line of six or eight pounds test on a tip-up equipped with a large reel that holds plenty of line and releases smoothly. For lakers I run that line through an egg sinker and tie it to a barrel swivel. To the barrel swivel I tie a leader two pounds test lighter than the main line, two or three feet long. The leader runs to a light-wire hook of about size 10 or 12.

Bait up with a blue or grey minnow or live smelt and fish just off bottom in waters 60 feet or deeper for lake trout and splake (the latter behaves much like its half-parent laker).

Lake trout fishing is among the most predictable of winter trout fisheries. Finding lakers is the toughest chore; they're usually willing to take practically any living or dead minnow or fish bait. It's a good idea to combine the efforts of your fishing party to stretch the legal number of tip-ups over as many depths as possible to locate the fish first. But at least lakers stay near bottom, which removes another question mark from the angler's mind.

You've a choice of several live baits when setting tip-ups for winter lake trout. Smelt make up a big part of their diets. If you can find them or catch them, they're deadly on lakers. Blue and gray minnows are good, too, but I've had little luck on golden shiners. One laker-fan friend catches big ciscoes and uses them dead as lake trout bait. He ices a few 20 pounders each winter.

How well do smelt work? An ice fishing friend and I often make special trips to a deep lake the night before a laker fishing trip, just to fish for our bait. Honestly, though, gray or blue shiners seem to work almost as well, and buying them in bait shops is far easier than catching your own smelt.

Whatever bait you use, hook it in under the dorsal (back) fin. That holds it level and keeps it alive and lively. Trout get hooked easily as they try to swallow the minnow.

I like to attach a small clip-on bobber to my tip-up line, just an inch or two below the set reel. Then if there's a flag, I can look for the bobber. If I can see it I know either the wind set the flag a-flying, the fish hit and dropped the bait, or the fish is hanging just below the hole. And I know where to re-set the line quickly.

But if the bobber's gone or, better yet, the reel is spinning, I know the fish has my bait. I'm never in a hurry to set the hook. Usually the small hooks will have caught in the fish's mouth or throat long before I've reached the tip-up.

Gently take the tip-up from the hole and peel a few more feet of line from it. Then set it in your minnow bucket so the reel won't freeze. Let the fish snug up the extra line or gently tighten it yourself, and set the hook. Now it's a hand-over-hand fight, and one in which the fish may often demand line. Be sure to allow the rather light line to slip through your fingers.

The fight goes better, too, if a partner walks your tip-up away from the hole as you gain line from the fish. That reduces the chances of tangling that long piece of light line. Your partner can be called back toward you if you need to feed more line to a running fish.

More trout are probably lost within a few feet of the hole than at any other point during the fight. Often an excited angler just doesn't react quickly enough when the fish makes another run. Some ice fishermen like a gaff hook to haul a big fish atop the ice. I don't. I'd rather let the fish make a few more runs, and then I will then start the fish's nose up the hole, grabbing it by hand and pulling it atop the ice. Gaffs may be efficient, but I'd rather lose a trout than poke a hole in it. And I've seen plenty of trout lost to improper or hasty gaffing, too.

A few tricks can boost your tip-up odds on lakers. One good one is lifting your tip-up a few feet in the air every 15 minutes or so. I don't know whether that movement coaxes a bite from a laker that might have been thinking about grabbing the minnow or if it just makes the bait more visible to fish in the vicinity, but I do know that half your day's flags may come within minutes of jigging the tip-ups. We've even lifted tip-ups to find a fish already on; it just didn't move far enough away to set off the flag.

Don't be afraid to move to deeper waters if your first choices don't pay off. In fact, never be afraid to move in the effort to locate lakers. (Just remember to keep checking the safety of the ice as you move across a lake.) We've learned to move any tip-up that doesn't produce after a half-hour or so. That keeps the boredome from getting to you and keeps alive the search for the day's hot hole. Often most of a day's catch will come from one tip-up, randomly set just where some aspect of bottom contour or supply of food has them concentrated. (You can sometimes even return to the same hole the next day for a fresh batch of laker action!)

Often lakers seem to haunt the relative shallows of waters 60 to 90 feet deep early and late in the ice season, and swim deeper in midwinter. We've caught them as deep as 175 feet in some large, deep Great Lakes Bays. Whatever the depth, keep your offering near bottom. Remember, most lakers are caught within a foot or two of bottom, and seldom are they found more than 10 feet above it.

Some lake trout fans swear by jigging or chugging methods. They chug heavy spoons and lures on hand-lines just off bottom in the same areas in which you'd set tip-ups for lakers. And they collect some nice catches. Lakers (and splake) will often slam a jigging-model Rapala minnow, lead-headed jig or other heavy spoons. The Swedish Pimple is a long-time favorite among laker fishermen everywhere. Many lures work better if baited or 'sweetened' with cut bait such as flesh from a sucker.

For bigger, baited lures you need stout rods and heavy line to provide enough hook-setting power, though, and you have to make sure your hook is sharp.

The heavy-lure approach to deep trout has spawned some interesting tackle in laker country. When fishing deep you must use a line with very little stretch. You want a tight line to impart the best action possible to the lure, and setting a big hook that far below you requires a solid, non-stretching connection. Some anglers find that low-stretching Dacron braided line works well, while others prefer a lead-core line or even wire line.

Seldom will a rod be used with such a rig; most fiberglass tips, after all, are overpowered by a hefty spoon and a stout line. So laker fans have fashioned such fishing tools as wooden, sickle-shaped sticks with pegs for holding their line. Others use a grooved stick 12 to 18 inches long on which their line can be wound. And still others manufacture donut-shaped wooden line holders; a groove around the out-side middle holds wound-on line, while the hole serves as a handle.

If using a relatively light lure like the Rapala or a lighter spoon — usually in shallower waters — you can get away with a reel-equipped rod, but a stick is often still preferable. There's little to go wrong in cold weather with a simple wooden stick; reels can sometimes freeze up, resulting in lost fish.

Keep your chugging lure near bottom. Most lakers, remember, are deep. And sometimes actually bouncing the lure on bottom seems to cause a ruckus that a laker just can't pass up. When they investigate and see your lure and bait impersonating a baitfish obviously crippled and unable to escape, the lazy, greedy lakers move in. Then you're in busi-ness. I like to keep the lure moving as much as possible, changing the rhythm until finding one that produces fish. Learn to feel what your lure is doing; many times the fish will take the lure as it flutters back down after a crisp lift upwards.

Strikes come in two forms — the explosive strike that can yank your knuckles down to ice-level, and a more subtle resistance that feels almost as if the trout is just gumming your lure. In either event you'll want sharp hook points to drive home, and care must be taken as the fish is fought topside. The heavier lure and line can fall free of the fish if you allow any slack. But in trade you can lean far more heavily into the fight of your fish than you could with lighter tackle.

Splake often behave like smaller versions of their laker parentage. (It takes a trained biologist in a laboratory, often, to distinguish between the two.) In general, however, splake will be found in slightly shallower water, and occasionally further off bottom, than lakers.

Splake will always have a hold on me, felt on my first ice fishing outing for trout. A friend took me along one early winter day. We settled on the ice over 40 feet of water, figuring we'd fish for perch with jigging rods there while watching tip-ups set for trout at a nearby dropoff into about water about 70 feet deep. We baited tear-drop lures with wax worms and lowered them on the jigging rods. My lure had barely reached bottom when it was gobbled, and the fight the 15-inch splake provided was exciting on the light rod. I was sold. The limit was then five trout per day of any species, and in a couple of hours we'd collected our 10 fish, the largest of them weighing almost four pounds.

Every year since we've returned to bore holes through the ice and that of other trout lakes, and we've usually been rewarded with members of one or more of the trout family. Splake methods were refined when we found minnows, day in and day out, far more productive than wax worms. You can offer splake two- to three-inch minnows effectively on either jigging rods or tip-ups.

The bottom-huggers — lakers and splake — are in many ways far different from brown trout, but variations on the tactics described above will also ice browns.

Brown trout are more difficult to find than lakers. Lakers are reliable, while it's often feast or famine on browns. Look for them, first of all, in the top 15 or 20 feet of water, whatever its depth. Browns are usually considered more skittish than lakers, too, so downsize your tackle.

For tip-up fishing for browns, I don't like line any heavier than four pounds test and insist upon a good-quality line, preferably clear. You can either rig special tip-ups for your

Figure 21 — A proud angler hoists a fat lake trout.

brown-trout fishing or simply add light leaders at least 10 feet long to your laker tip-ups.

Set the tip-up as lightly as possible so the fish doesn't feel too much resistance when it takes the bait. Substitute a small split shot or two for the egg sinker used for lakers, adding only enough weight to keep the bait — blue or grey minnows two or three inches long — down. Attach a small clip-on bobber just below the set reel to make it easy to return to the bait to the same depth after (hopefully) catching a brown. And set tip-ups away from the area where you'll be sitting to keep your ice-top commotion from spooking the fish. We've caught them at weights of up to eight pounds using that approach.

Re-read the earlier section on fighting lake trout. The same principles apply to tip-up caught browns. Browns, in my opinion, are even more explosive fighters than lakers, so be extra cautious. Repeated runs make alertness necessary. And many a belligerent brown has been lost hole-side when an impatient angler tried to ice it too soon.

Jigging works on brown trout, too, but the fishing is different. Browns are funny when you have become used to catching bottom-hugging lakers, and not many anglers jig for them when they're suspended over deeper waters.

A partner and I once stumbled onto a brown trout bonanza that still makes me smile. We'd heard that orange jigging-model Rapalas were good for perch and browns, and decided to try for some perch along a deepwater dropoff on a two-story lake, one that held both coolwater (perch, bass and pike) and coldwater (trout) species. The eight-inch-thick, clear ice was rumbling, making more ice yet on this 10-degree day, as we began lowering lures 40 feet to the bottom. And when the lures reached bottom, we often caught a perch on them — unless a trout got there first!

The browns were following a common winter pattern, cruising 15 to 20 feet below the ice. Sometimes they'd stop a lure as it was being lowered, sometimes they'd slam one as it was being brought top-side for a check. More escaped than were caught, but we iced several nice ones. The splake,

Figure 22 — Look for brown trout in the top 15 to 20 feet of water, regardless of the water depth.

many of them about a foot long, were evidently swimming among the perch, and it became a guessing game as to which fish — a perch or trout — would come up with the lure.

Now we never head onto a trout lake without a few of the Rapalas, and more than once they've provided action on a slow day, either on trout or perch. A short spinning rod and open face reel works well for this light-action jigging. The drag allows you to hook and play a big fish on light line. For browns, use a good four- or six-pound test line, especially if your reel has a reliable drag. The quick retrieve of a reel is a blessing when bringing up fish from depths of up to 100 feet!

Leave the traditional heavy sticks and wire line home if jigging for brown trout. The heavy line with which they're wrapped will spook the more-wary browns. Six-pound test will work on browns; if you're careful you'll find your action improving with four-pound test. Try lighter spoons, smaller Swedish Pimples or jigging-model Rapalas in size 5 or 7 and, especially, in the bright orange finish.

For any brown trout fishing, keep ice-top commotion to a minimum, since browns often appear to avoid sounds of spudding, power augers and snowmobiles.

Regular spinning tackle can also be used for any of the salmonid (trout or salmon) species. Light line is favored, and the rod is propped up with the bail open so a fish can take out line freely. For browns or Atlantic salmon use a bobber to keep the bait at the desired depth. Fish the bottom for lakers and splake. Spinning tackle offers the best of both tip-up and jigging worlds. Leave the bait at rest, as with a tip-up. You don't have a flag to call you to action and will thus have to watch for line peeling off the reel. But in return you can enjoy a free-wheeling fight of a big fish on a light-action rod. Your fishing success rate may not go up, but your fishing enjoyment just might increase.

Spinning-rod ice fishing provided interesting angling for a trout-fishing friend of mine several seasons ago. Tom was fishing shallow water for brown trout on a big inland lake, using ultra-light spinning tackle.

"I was fishing about five feet down in 10 feet of water," he told me later with a laugh. "I got two hits and caught two fish. My partner also caught one. We thought they looked a little unusual, but we were sure they were brown trout, so we took them home and ate them."

Later Tom got thinking again about the unusual appearances of the 6-pound and 4½-pound fish he'd eaten. Browns have squared tails and the tails of these fish were slightly forked. The spots on the sides were a little different than those on most brown trout, too, and the fish turned blue-grey as they lay on the ice, instead of assuming the darker tones normally seen in dying brown trout.

He mentioned his doubts to a couple of fellow-anglers and they suggested that, just maybe, the fish could have been Atlantic salmon. That thought had crossed his mind, too, but he hadn't heard of any releases of those fish, close cousins to brown trout and often difficult to distinguish from them.

"Then," Tom said, "I found out that the Department of Natural Resources had planted 1,600 Atlantics in that lake two years earlier, and that they would have been about the size of the ones we caught. I could have kicked myself. I wanted a nice Atlantic salmon to (have mounted and) put on the wall."

Grumbling but determined, Tom returned to the lake a few days later. Sure enough, he caught another Atlantic salmon, this one a 4½-pounder, and sped it to a taxidermist.

Tom had his trophy, but the story will haunt him. Now when he catches a fish, of whatever type, his friends regularly question his identification of it. He still smiles, however — for he does have a mounted Atlantic salmon on his wall.

In some lakes brook trout are legal year-around, and fishing for them in winter is a delicate, enjoyable pursuit. I remember laying on my belly on a small inland lake, watching a waxworm-baited tear-drop on four-pound test line as it bobbed three feet down in clear waters four feet deep. Occasionally the snout of a brightly-colored brookie poked out and the trout, with a sudden burst of speed, would attack the bait. Sometimes I'd be quick enough setting the hook and flipped the trout onto the snowy ice, but more often the fish would hit and run, sometimes with my bait, while I was left laying in the snow, a smile pasted on my face. It's generally hard to find lakes open for winter brookie fishing, however.

Not so with rainbow trout. Many lakes, large and small, offer planted populations of 'bows, and they'll fall for a variety of ice-fishing methods.

If you fish for panfish, you're ready to try for rainbows. Fish within six feet of bottom, using a limber rod lined with monofilament of two or four pounds test. Good lures include tear-drops, ice flies and small spoons. Bait them with waxworms, corn borers, wigglers, small minnows, crayfish or salmon eggs. Corn is a long-time favorite of rainbow anglers, too.

If your state allows it, chumming with corn, salmon eggs or even oatmeal often boosts the action. There are several ways to offer this chum efficiently.

Some anglers simply fill a paper lunch bag with corn or eggs, and tie the closed bag to a long string or fishing line. The bag sinks (add weight if necessary) and, once on bottom, tears open with a sharp tug from above. The trout quickly find this source of food — plus the hooked food you're offering them.

You can also build a chumming bucket from an old one-pound coffee can. Attach a cord to a ring soldered on the bottom of the can, then tie a cotter pin onto the cord about a foot higher. Slip the cotter pin onto the top edge of the can and fill it with bait. The bucket will sink bottom-down, and a sharp tug on the line will pull the cotter pin free and turn the pail bottoms-up.

Many ice anglers find night-fishing to be most productive for rainbows, and they use artificial light. In shallow water or on clear ice a lantern near your fishing hole may draw fish closer. Some fishermen even use 12-volt lights, protected from the water in a sealed glass jar, lowered to fish level to attract trout. (The same trick often works on crappies!)

Most winter trout (and salmon) lakes offer fish planted by

conservation departments. Usually released at fingerling length, the trout quickly find new homes in coldwater lakes, making good use of the forage fish available. Browns may begin showing up in the catch just a year or two later, while lakers take longer to mature.

Some biologists say lakers must be at least three years old before they really start showing up in the catch, and then only in the 14- to 18-inch range. Some really big lakers from cold, clear water — the trophy 20-pounders that make news everywhere — may be 20 years old. Rainbows provide fishing action within a year or two of release.

Begin your trout-lake research by checking with local fish biologists to learn which lakes have been planted with trout, and when.

And when winter moves in and drives late-season boat fishermen off your favorite lake, wait only until the ice is good and safe, and then head onto it.

Figure 23 — Varying the quarry or approach can often lead to more ice fishing fun.

Chapter 11

Etc.

How often have you finished a day's ice fishing and begun gathering up all your equipment again, only to find that it won't fit in the container in which you carried it out?

Somehow, once you got really involved in the fishing, things just kind of spread out. Some of the lures are back in their boxes, some not. The tip-ups are iced-up and won't fold back up as compactly as when you began. Happily, you collected a few fish, and they're taking up some of the room taken by the gear on the walk out.

The upshot is that you've got some loose ends — stuff that just doesn't seem to fit anywhere else.

That's what this chapter is. We've included bits and pieces of ice-fishing lore that don't really come under the other chapter headings in the table of contents. Still, they're important and enjoyable parts of ice fishing.

SPEARING

The best-known quarry of the winter spearer is the northern pike, and many are the pike impaled upon spears each winter across the ice region, their captors opening the door of a warm shanty to toss the trophies onto the ice.

Hunger is the pike's undoing. The spearer usually hangs a decoy — either a live sucker about six inches long or more, or an artificial replica of a game or food fish.

(I've got a bunch of old fishing tackle — stuff I really treasure — and my favorites are a half-dozen old spearing decoys that some ingenius angler carved from driftwood, adding aluminum fins and primitive paint. You can tell the alleged brook trout from the likely sucker, but the fact that both worked reduces my fear of failing at spearing because of a faulty decoy!)

Spearers who use live bait report one big advantage. They say that an active sucker — which they'll use for several days if possible — will 'freeze' when a northern comes on the scene, allowing the angler to ready his spear even before the pike comes into view. It's a three-way war of nerves between the northern, the decoy and the angler.

To an observer, spearing might seem casual — waiting comfortably in a dark shanty until a pike appears below, then poking it with a spear. But there's far more to it than that; you've got to be a knowledgeable, patient and alert angler to succeed at this sport.

The first requirement for successful spearing is darkness. And since pike are active almost exclusively in the daytime, it's up to you to make sure your fishing shanty is light-proof. Every window must be covered and every seam and corner sealed. Now make sure your stove, if you have one, doesn't throw any light.

(Make sure, though, that while barring the light, your shanty provides good ventilation; don't give oxygen loss or carbon monoxide a chance to end your life.)

Your spearing coop must also be quiet. Get surplus gear out of the way, where you won't be banging it around. A piece of old carpet on the floor can cut noise further. Old-time spearers even advise newcomers to the sport to wear dark-colored clothes. Do everything you can to ensure that you'll see the pike and that he won't see you.

Each spear fisherman has his own favorite spear design. Here, though, are some general guidelines. Make it a weighted spear so you don't have to throw it too hard. Make sure it has from seven to nine tines and is about seven feet long. You'll want a rope attached to it, too.

Here's a rope-rigging tip from the Michigan Department of Natural Resources: "Run your rope through a cotterpin on the spear's handle down to the tines where it is tied fast or secured with a metal ring. When you hit the mark and start to haul the fish in, a slight jerk pulls the cotterpin out and lets you lift the spear with the tines up. If the fish is not speared very well, this helps to keep it on the tines instead of giving it a chance to work free."

Other tricks can help, like keeping the spear's tines just underwater at all times, or at least slipping them in prior to tossing the spear. If you throw it in one movement from above the water, the pop and splash may well send the pike on its way long before the spear gets to it.

Maybe the hardest thing about spear-fishing is cutting the hole through which you watch for the fish. An auger just won't work, leaving you the choice of a spud, axe or chain saw. As the winter fishing season lengthens, the task of hole-cutting gets tougher.

And there's another matter related to holes used for spearing — mark them well when you leave. In my part of the country a branch or piece of brush stuck in the snow is a universal signal of an abandoned fishing hole, and we stay clear. Leaving an unmarked hole can have tragic consequences for an angler, skater or snowmobiler coming along later — especially if it's a large spearing hole. Mark it well, even if it requires a long hike to shore for a suitable marker. It's a major responsibility, and a small price to pay for the pleasure of tending a spearing hole.

Pike aren't the only target of the spear, either. In many states muskellunge are legal quarry, and the same tactics take them as are used for pike.

Figure 24 — This sturgeon — 76½ pounds and 66½ inches long — was speared by the angler at right. A fish biologist, left, inspects the catch.

SPEAR A STURGEON?

Even sturgeon are speared each winter, although usually only from designated lakes and during special seasons. Your best bet there is to hire the services of a guide, or at least rent a shanty already in place over productive sturgeon-spearing grounds.

These behemoths — some of them well over 100 pounds — call for specialized tackle and techniques. And since they're relatively scarce, you need to spend your hours and days over areas used by these prehistoric-appearing fish.

The most popular sturgeon-spearing approach is to lower a wooden, plastic or metal decoy into water about 20 feet deep, then wait for curiousity to bring the big fish into spearing range. The decoy, apparently, doesn't resemble anything in the fish's diet. "They feed primarily on wigglers, fingernail clams, crayfish and some aquatic plants," a fish biologist told me. "They have a sucking-type mouth, and have no provisions for chewing food."

Don't expect to see a "normal-looking" fish swim into view when you're huddled in a sturgeon-spearing shanty. Physically, biologists say, the sturgeon is a holdover from prehistoric times and is believed to have evolved about a hundred million years ago. Its big, shark-like tail, bony body and long, rubbery snout (with feelers suspended underneath, yet!) all together create one of the strangest sights an angler can view.

But their meat is rated excellent when smoked or fried, their eggs can be used as caviar, and even their bladders can be made into a pure form of gelatin used in jellies.

The sturgeon now receives far more respect than it did a century ago when commercial fishermen on the Great Lakes cursed the big net-wreckers. Thousands of sturgeon, according to published reports, were stacked on beaches, dried and burned.

WHITEFISH JIGGING

Lake trout and lake (or 'common') whitefish are natural winter neighbors, haunting the same deepwater holes in winter. So ice fishing for whitefish is a deepwater proposition.

Take another look at the tips we provided for jigging for lake trout in the trout fishing chapter; we'll be altering them only slightly for whitefishing.

Most whitefish anglers use traditional methods, chugging heavy Swedish Pimples on low-stretch Dacron line. The line is simply wound around a stick, which is then used as a primitive jigging rod. I have one friend who, despite lots of more refined tackle, still believes the rough chugging stick does the best job. "I think I catch more fish with a stick," he says. "I have a little more control over the lure and can give it just the action I want. I can twitch it and barely move it. I just get a better feel of what's going on down there."

Figure 25 — Jigging for deepwater whitefish can be cold, but fans say the tasty fish are worth the effort.

And the Dacron line, with its reduced stretch, makes it far easier to set the hook in a fish as much as 150 feet below you.

A good combination is 18-pound test Dacron, with a six-foot leader of 12- to 17-pound test monofilament running to the lure.

If building your own stick, here's a trick. Make the stick exactly two or three feet long; that way you can keep track of which depth is most productive. Most whitefish fisheries begin relatively shallow when ice first forms, moving deeper as winter deepens and shallower again as spring approaches. Yesterday's success is your best clue for today's fishing.

In really bitter weather, you're best off to leave the chugging sticks home, though. That's when a short spinning rod, equipped with an open-face spinning reel loaded with eight- or ten-pound test monofilament, really does the trick.

Setting the hook with the spinning outfit is a little more difficult, but it's far easier to keep the line tight — about an even trade-off. And the ability to spool line onto a reel instead of laying a hopeless tangle of braided line on the ice is really appreciated in cold, blustery weather.

Whitefish techniques are really quite simple. White Swedish Pimples in size seven are most popular, sometimes dressed up with a green or red dot or a colored or silver "flicker" on the lower split ring. Some whitefish experts add a barrel swivel between the hook and lure, to extend the reach of the hook a little. Others add another treble hook to the split ring at the top of the lure. I've brought several whitefish to the top, the top hook securely in their mouths and the factory-installed hooks dangling free.

Some days the whitefish really seem to respond to the addition of skeined eggs from trout, salmon, whitefish or even perch. Tied spawn bags don't seem quite as successful.

A soft jigging action of a foot or so seems most effective; use milder strokes than you would for lake trout. (And don't be surprised if your catch mixes lake trout and whitefish, since they favor the same areas.)

Whitefish, while not strictly a schooling fish, often congregate around food sources. Start over about 90 feet of water, and try chugging the lure 50 or 75 times. If there's no action, move, and keep moving deeper until you either find fish or give up. You can, if it's legal where you fish, cultivate your own fishing hotspot by chumming with corn, fish eggs or even fish scales.

Finding the whitefish in the first place can be the biggest challenge. And my whitefish-fan friend offers a tip that can help. Remember that whitefish are very popular with anglers (and fish-eaters!). So watch other fishermen. "If one guy is in the same spot for very long, I become suspicious. If I'm in a wandering mood and not catching fish, I go over," relates my friend.

Figure 26 — It won't win any beauty contests, but the burbot, a freshwater cod, offers game fights and good eating.

BURBOT: UGLY IS ONLY SKIN DEEP?

If you fish for lake trout long enough in one of the big, deep lakes in which they're native, sooner or later you're likely to catch a burbot. I guarantee you won't forget your first one.

The burbot is also called the ling, ling cod, lawyer or cusk. It is the only member of the cod family to swim in fresh water, and its taste is considered very close to the saltwater cod.

Before you can enjoy that taste, however, you must get by its appearance — unusual at best, perhaps even ugly.

The body is long and relatively slender, at least once past the rib bone structures. The head is large, relatively flat, and features three barbels. It has two dorsal fins, one running back almost to the tail. It is greenish-black in color and, when brought up from the depths at which it normally swims, the eel-like body often coils from the change in pressure.

Most burbot are caught incidentally by anglers trying for lake trout or, less frequently, walleyes. The ling cod generally haunt waters frequented by lake trout, those in the 80 to 200 foot depths. But lawyers have been found in depths of 700 feet — and as shallow as one to four feet at spawning time, which comes under the last ice of the season.

Biologists say most feeding by burbot takes place at night, although these greedy feeders will often set a tip-up flag a-flying at mid-day, too. They like fish, crayfish and other organic foods. They'll readily chomp on the minnows or smelt you offer lake trout — either alive or dead. Once hooked they wage an impressive battle, at least as gamely as a lake trout.

Burbot offer plenty of resistance when they're at bottom, and sometimes the fish just can't be budged by the angler above. As the fish is brought topside, however, the change in pressure removes some of the zip from the fish, and odds quickly turn in the angler's favor.

And despite their unique (ugly?) appearance, some

anglers prize them for the table. The flesh is firm, white and very mild-flavored, low in oil and relatively free of bones. Their large livers, which some regard as very tasty, are high in vitamins A and D.

I've caught burbot (and seen them caught) on Great Lakes bays and from larger, coldwater inland lakes. The fish is interesting — but more interesting are the reactions of the anglers who catch them. Some anglers kill burbot and leave them on the ice for the seagulls; but others call them "gentlemen's catfish" and happily collect them for the dinner table.

"I'd almost as soon have a lawyer as a trout," one regular lake-trout angler told me one day, as he iced his fourth burbot of the day.

A fisheries biologist told me, "Burbot are a tremendous fish. They have an awfully large liver, and the liver is a real delicacy, probably the best part of the fish." He said the liver can be cooked by rolling it in a batter and deep-fat-frying it, just like other fish.

The long tail is lined with clean, white meat, which, cut into narrow strips and boiled in salted water, tastes quite a bit like lobster or other seafood. Frying the fillets is also popular.

The best way to catch a burbot is to go after lake trout. But while lakers can often be found anywhere in the first 10 feet of water off bottom, the burbot is almost always right on bottom.

SMELT

What is the smallest fish to consistently draw the interest of ice fishermen? I'm betting it's the smelt, which has plenty of fans for two very good reasons. The smelt is one of the deadliest baits for lake trout, splake and northern pike fishing. And fried smelt — especially those caught in winter — are a tasty delight.

In my Great Lakes neighborhood spring is considered to have arrived once large schools of smelt gather along the Great Lakes shoreline for their spring spawning runs. They're

Figure 27 — Panfish tackle, a gas lantern for light and a cooler to hold fish are all that's required for catching smelt for bait or a meal.

met there by wader-clad anglers with hand nets; in some areas dip nets or even seines are allowed. And buckets of smelt are collected. Too many anglers get smelt fever and keep more than they can eat or clean, leaving them with a surplus to give away or bury.

You're not apt to collect catches of that magnitude through the ice, but I think you'll agree you get a better quality of fish in the winter. They seem firmer, with a finer tasting meat. And that's if you plan to eat them; if you have a big-game fishing trip coming, the best bait in the world is in your bucket.

Many pike fishermen, along with those after several trout species, already know that a live smelt will often outfish about any other bait they can offer. A dead smelt is a close second.

You may at first find it ironic to fish for your bait. My own dad, years after first learning about our nighttime smelt-fishing trips, still laughs aloud when he tells people that his son, allegedly of sound mind, drives an hour to a deep lake to fish half the night for smelt — just so he can drive to another deep lake the next day with a fresh supply of bait for lake trout fishing.

Almost all smelt fishing takes place at night, and most of it from shanties equipped with large reels that allow a fish to be iced quickly and the bait relowered. Most of these special reels use two spools on the same axle. The larger holds the fishing line, the smaller is attached to a cord. When you lower the fishing line the axle turns, winding up the heavier cord. Pulling on the cord, then, wraps the fishing line back onto the larger wheel. These devices can easily be made at home (a bicycle wheel works well), or purchased at bait shops near smelt-fishing lakes.

The portable angler, however, can find good success fishing in the open at night, with little more than his bluegill fishing tackle. Start with a portable gasoline lantern. Drill your fishing holes and pile up the resulting slush in the center of the pattern of holes, usually four holes about six feet apart for two anglers. The slush will provide a platform for your lantern.

Four-pound test monofilament line is fine. Many smelt fishermen bait small hooks or tear-drop-shaped lures with small, "pin-head" minnows, but I've had nearly as much luck with wax worms or other grubs, and they're a lot easier to handle.

If you're actually seeking the smaller smelt (five inches long or less) for bait, wax worms may in fact be a better bet. Until smelt reach lengths of five or six inches, biologists say, their diet consists mainly of small plants and animals, crustaceans, worms and insects. After that they begin to rely more on fish.

Some states allow smelt anglers — fishing on known smelt lakes — to use more than the usual number of hooks. By spreading out several baits on one line, you can more quickly determine the depth at which smelt are found on a certain night. Best winter concentrations of smelt are often near bottom in 40 feet of water, although good catches from 10 to 60 feet down are common.

Get your smelt atop the ice quickly if you'll be using them for bait. Have a cooler ready, filled with water from the lake in which you're fishing. At home, an aquarium-type aerator helps keep them alive. If some die, keep them frozen solid in a freezer for another fishing trip. Dead smelt often out-catch live minnows.

None of those concerns are real if you're planning to cook up a midwinter mess of smelt. Once you do, however, you may not go back to store-bought or spring-caught smelt.

SPIN-FISHING

We've concentrated on three major types of ice fishing throughout this book — jigging with light, panfish tackle; tending tip-ups for larger gamefish; and chugging heavy lures for the larger, predatory species. But spin-fishing is another option for the ice angler as interested in the challenge as in the catch.

A friend of mine is a commercial builder of custom fishing rods. He specializes in rods for open-water fishing for salmon, and trout, especially steelhead trout. So when Tom Hodges of Midland, Mich., goes ice fishing for pike, walleyes, trout and salmon, you couldn't expect him to grab traditional ice gear, could you? He doesn't. Instead, he uses five-foot, ultra-light graphite spinning rods, open-face spinning reels and eight-pound test line.

Of course, there's no casting possible on the ice and, unless you're fishing right on the bottom or you're willing to hold the rod all day, you'll have to depend on a bobber or float to hold your offering at the right depth. When weather is fair, try a two-bobber system. A bobber just large enough to hold the weight and bait aloft sits on the water. A smaller, preferably sliding-type bobber is out of the water. When it disappears, you know you have a fish on.

Removing a bobber can be difficult when fighting a fish. When fishing shallow Hodges ties on a small swivel, adding a leader as long as the depth of the water in which he'll be fishing. He leaves a tag end on the swivel and clips the bobber to it. Then the bobber can simply be slid off during the fight. If fishing a straight line the bobber can be unsnapped from the line by the fisherman or a partner.

If the weather is foul the two-bobber system doesn't work as well. Under those conditions slide a rubber band onto the handle of the rod and tuck a loop of line under it, leaving the bail of the reel open. A fish's bite pulls the loop of line free and the quarry can run without feeling resistance.

The eight-pound-test mainline is a good start, but for many species you can boost catches by running a lighter leader from it, ending in a size 12 or 14 treble hook below just enough weight to keep the minnow down.

The ultra-light spinning approach offers some of the most exciting fights of the winter season. There are drawbacks — you must stay closer to your fishing holes to detect a bite, for one — but some anglers find them outweighed by the extra excitement of a light-tackle fight with a big fish.

Chapter 12

Ice Fisherman's Sunset

A frozen lake knows when sundown is coming. Several hours before dark it begins to tighten, rumbling thunderously as changing temperatures shift the ice. Anglers stir, too, as the sun that shone so brightly all afternoon now dips in the southwest and chilling breezes blow across the frozen expanse.

What a day it has been. "Wonder what the rich folks did today?" one buddy muses aloud, as he kicks warmth back into slightly numbed toes. "If they're smart, they're out here somewhere," another responds, pointing across the big, frozen lake. Everything's just right. The walk back to the car or cabin is just long enough to build up a warming head of steam. We don't have buckets filled with minnows to lug along. And even though the fish we've caught far outweigh those early-morning minnows, somehow they're far less a load.

We've watched an entire day unfold on this winter lake, each section of that day a separate memory. Together they form a master's quiltwork of pleasure.

Figure 28 — A father-and-son team combine to fight a lake trout.

This morning we stood at the edge of the lake, pulling on heavy clothes (and yelling at one adventurer to close the van door while the rest of us donned boots and snowmobile suits.) Each of us gathered more gear than we could ever need, each of us still forgetting at least one piece of equipment we really could use. Buckets and boxes filled with tip-ups, jig rods, lures and terminal tackle. A bag of cheese and nuts in one of them, a vacuum bottle of coffee in another. I stashed two cameras in a fanny pack wrapped around my waist and carried a minnow bucket in hand. You pulled a sled laden with a power auger.

The kid — yours, and just nicely 12 years old — grabbed whatever was left and made self-consciously sure that he lugged his fair share.

Onto the lake, then. Walking, as it always seems, into the wind. The crispness takes your breath away a minute, and oft-clogged winter noses quickly loosen. You can sometimes tell what kind of day it's going to be by the way your face feels on the way out.

If your cheeks smart just a little, it's from dry cold. The air is clear, so there's little chance of snow or, worse yet, rain. We were half-way to the area we wanted to fish and no breath froze on my moustache. That meant it was warmer than 10 degrees below zero. (Remember the walleye-fishing day on the frozen waters of a river impoundment when my breath froze into solid ice, welding moustache to beard so firmly that, three hours into the fishing, I couldn't get my mouth open wide enough to eat a sandwich? We found out later it was 30 degrees below zero.)

If there's wetness in the air, there are two possibilities. One is that snow is coming. Maybe by noon it will be difficult to spot our furthest tip-ups. And chances are we'd then pack up early enough to get home before dark, even on slippery roads. Maybe it will be warm and damp, that combination that lets you leave your gloves off but keeps you from kneeling in the sloppy snow.

The sun peeping over the horizon gives more weather clues. Today it was clear and bright, along with the sky

Figure 29 — Victorious, father and son display a nice lake trout — the son's first.

around it. I bet then, based upon past experience, that our best action would come from daybreak to 9 a.m., then again from 3 p.m. to dark. Again, I was wrong.

It was almost noon when Chuck, that 12-year-old of yours, spied the tip-up flag being released even before it was freely flying. He was off his bucket seat even before we knew anything was afoot. He was ready to fight a trout.

The trout was ready, too, spinning the reel madly as it made for water even deeper than the 100 feet in which the bait was hung. Like a pro Chuck lifted the tip-up carefully from the hole, setting it in the minnow bucket he'd grabbed on his way. (He's a clear-thinker; most of the time we forget to grab the bucket and have to send someone back for it.) Putting the reel underwater keeps it from freezing during the fight, and makes re-rigging far easier.

As he set the tip-up aside Chuck deftly spun a few more yards of line off the reel, leaving some slack between him and the fish. When the fish took up that slack Chuck yanked the hook home and began the fight.

I snapped pictures as you and Chuck bent over the hole, you giving him a few pointers on snaking in monofilament line hand-over-hand and he tolerant enough to accept those tips. When the fish finally came into view he eased it closer to the hole in the ice while you dropped your gloves in the snow and rolled up your sleeves. The fish tired and Chuck started the big lake trout's head up through the hole. You grabbed it around what would have been its neck if it had one. Just that quickly the seven-pounder flopped onto the ice, staining the snow with a few drops of crimson blood — a splash of sadness on a field of cheery white. Quietly Chuck pulled the hook out of this, his first big trout, then carried the fish 20 feet away from the hole. You and I both silently watched him as he lay the dying fish in the snow, gently wiping away the blood and slush from its green and grey body.

You and I, buddy, have caught a lot of fish from a lot of winter lakes. We've caught them fishing as a two-man team. We've caught them in parties of a half-dozen anglers. Some of our partners will fish with us no more, taken from us between ice seasons. Others have less tragically drifted off to different sports, different spots or different friends.

I can't think of a fish I enjoyed more than the one Chuck caught today — a fish in whose capture I really had no part. I was flattered when Chuck used some of the tricks we taught him, impressed with the classy touches he provided himself. And uplifted with the reverence he showed the fish — proud to have taken it, with none of that adolescent thrill-of-the-kill that's exhibited by too damned many anglers of all ages.

It's kind of sad, maybe, to think that this youngster has passed the stage when ice fishing meant running across a frozen lake, sliding in the snow like a baserunner stealing third. Now he's one of the team. He'll stand back the next time a tip-up flag flies and there's another newcomer with us; he'll let the new guy take the first fish. God, he might even start drilling the holes for us, his angling companions getting (in his eyes) so advanced in years. When we're gone he might even tell the kind of stories on us that we've told him on others.

Yes, this is an especially sweet sundown, even though we're buzzing down the highway as the orb finally dips below the horizon. We'll let Chuck watch for deer along the two-lane this time; it's a good incentive for him to keep eyes open instead of dozing in the back of the van.

The miles tick off, the tape in the deck sings softly. There's little talking among our trio of anglers, probably for at least a couple of reasons.

One, there's little left to be said. This morning, along this same highway, we chatted incessantly, hatching plots against the well-being of every fish in the big lake. Minnows and breakfasts and tackle all blended into the verbal collage. But that was before those theories had been tested, those minnows offered and the food burned in coldweather activity. Now we've had cold air fuel-injected into our lungs, eyes and souls, and the return to warmth has brought on a heavy dose of drowsiness. Thanks again, bud, for staying awake while I drive.

(Chuck's sitting on the van's bed, and I swear I just saw him lean over to brush the snow off that trout of his one more time.)

Home, we'll spread our fish out on newspapers and fillet them, taking care not to let sleepiness leave us sliced by a knife. I'm going to fry up a couple of chunks and freeze the rest. No, maybe not. Frozen fish never tastes as good as fresh, so I'll make a few stops tonight or tomorrow and pass out some fish to the friends and relatives who listen to our ice-talk all year.

The pattern's the same, after all, year after year. About July, when the temperatures first poke into those unbearable 90s, we wait for the next batch of cool weather. When it arrives we burst in on unsuspecting golfers, waterskiers or picnickers, advising them that it's "making ice." Those around us shake their heads, diving back into a swimming pool or watermelon.

They don't understand, after all, that ice fishing is a year-around state of mind. The melt of ice may begin in February but in my mind it lasts through midsummer, until the lake hits its seasonal temperature peak. Past that high point it's in the process of making ice, even if that solid water doesn't show for five months.

I know your car has perch-fishing spoons in the glove compartment all year. There's a battered jigging rod that never leaves the storage space under my van's bed.

Maybe, though, we are a little crazy. I'm talking to myself silently, you're watching the woods along the road, and Chuck's watching his fish.

Here's the ski slope next to the highway. We each crane our necks to see how many neon-clad Alpiners are afoot there. The parking lot's full again. The skiers are kindred souls, since they're outdoor- and winter-minded. And I'm selfishly glad they're clustered on these man-made hills instead of on our favorite lake. But it would be neat to see how they'd react to a day of our sport.

The outdoors is never so magical as on a frozen lake, where smoke from a wood stove is more visible than the cabin from which it issues. Where the only clues to fish are those in your mind. Where neither partner in a fish-landed handshake can feel the hand of the other through thick gloves.

It's a magical world anglers share on every frozen lake, and there's room for more.

Plenty of room, that is, if they're the right anglers.

Remember the handbill we found plastered on our windshield along the warmwater lake just a few miles from home? We'd parked the car on the road and walked down the hill for years, vaguely aware that it was legally an access site only for residents of the subdivision, not everyone. These folks had been nice and allowed literally hundreds of anglers to slide down the steep bank onto the lake, year after year.

"Dear Fishermen," the handbill began. "The folks who live in this subdivision would like your help.

"We believe that people should enjoy the lake and we like to see people having a good time.

"We have, however, a problem that a FEW people are causing us. Most of the fishermen try to be considerate and cooperative with the property owners of the subdivision.

"The heavy snows have created even more of a parking problem. If cars are parked at the corner of the drive and the lane other cars have difficulty getting around the corner. The school bus has had to back out and onto the road because the driver could not get the bus around the corner.

"We ask that you not park near the mailboxes, block the driveways or park across from a driveway. Please try to park on just one side of the roadway.

"The access at the corner is not a public access. This access is owned by the residents on the west side of the road so that they have a right-of-way to the lake.

"People who are not residents of the subdivision have been permitted to reach the lake through the access. We hope we can continue this.

"Some believe the subdivision to be their personal dumping grounds for bottles, cans, trash, papers and ashtrays. Look at the litter left on the lake. Those bottles and cans are going to float into swimming areas this summer, causing more cut feet on children.

"A few have found it clever to use obscenities toward the women and children on the street.

"Remember the guy that found it necessary to spud three holes in the middle of a small area cleared of snow so that the children could ice skate?

"We don't want to have to fence off the access, and we certainly don't want to go to war with the fishermen that come up for a good time and try to be considerate neighbors.

"We only ask that the fishermen be considerate of us. Please drive carefully for the sake of the small children who live here. Give us the same consideration that you would want us to give your families and your property in your neighborhood.

"Thank you for helping.

"The subdvision folks."

We were embarassed reading that letter, ashamed of fellow-fishermen and secretly afraid that maybe we'd blocked a driveway or cussed a little louder than necessary.

But setting the letter down on the seat of the car, I saw your kid Chuck, then just 10 years old. The bluegill fishing had been slow, and he'd become a little bored. In 15 minutes he'd carefully gathered a handful of trash left by others. He had carried it back to the car, and now smiled to himself as he looked from the letter to the litter.

One of the best things about an ice fisherman's sundown, after all, just might be the clues it gives of an even better fishing day tomorrow.

Index